MADE TO
CRAVE
ACTION PLAN

Also by Lysa TerKeurst

Am I Messing Up My Kids?

Becoming More Than a Good Bible Study Girl

Becoming More Than a Good Bible Study Girl video curriculum

Capture His Heart (for wives)

Capture Her Heart (for husbands)

Leading Women to the Heart of God

Living Life on Purpose

Made to Crave

Made to Crave Devotional

Made to Crave for Teens

Made to Crave video curriculum

What Happens When Women Say Yes to God

What Happens When Women Say Yes to God video curriculum

What Happens When Women Walk in Faith

Who Holds the Key to Your Heart?

Also by Floyd H. "Ski" Chilton

The Gene Smart Diet

Inflammation Nation

Win the War Within

MADE TO CRAVE ACTION PLAN

YOUR JOURNEY TO HEALTHY LIVING

SIX SESSIONS

LYSA TERKEURST
& DR. SKI CHILTON
WITH CHRISTINE M. ANDERSON

ZONDERVAN®

ZONDERVAN.com/
AUTHORTRACKER
follow your favorite authors

ZONDERVAN

Made to Crave Action Plan Participant's Guide
Copyright © 2011 by Lysa TerKeurst and Dr. Ski Chilton

Requests for information should be addressed to:

Zondervan, *Grand Rapids, Michigan 49530*

ISBN 978-0-310-68441-1

Published in association with the literary agency of Fedd & Company, Inc., Post Office Box 341973, Austin, TX 78734.

Cover design: Rob Monacelli
Cover photography: Getty Image®
Interior design: Ben Fetterley

Printed in the United States of America

14 15 16 17 18 /DCI/ 22 21 20 19 18 17 16 15 14 13 12 11 10 9 8 7 6 5 4

Contents

About the Study

Eat carbs. Don't eat carbs.

Low fat is good. Low fat is bad.

Eat fish. But not that fish.

Good gracious, it's no wonder so many of us throw in the towel on healthy eating before we even get started. So much of the information out there is confusing at best and contradictory at worst. Well, exhale, my friend—the *Made to Crave Action Plan* is exactly what you've been looking for.

I understand how hard it is to tackle this issue of healthy eating. I wrote about my own food battles in the book, *Made to Crave: Satisfying Your Deepest Desire with God, Not Food*. As I wrote the book, I knew people had access to lots of *how-to* information about healthy eating. But I also knew there was a missing link, what I called the *want-to*—the emotional and spiritual motivation to make lasting changes.

When *Made to Crave* was published, I was overwhelmed by the positive response. People really resonated with it on a deep level. And then they started asking for more: "We understand this is a want-to book, but could you also give us some how-to information?"

That's when I invited Dr. Floyd "Ski" Chilton to join me for a six-week web cast. I chose Dr. Chilton because he is the author of several books on diet and wellness—including the critically acclaimed *Inflammation Nation*—and because he is a man of strong faith. Each week I focused on the *want-to*—the emotional and spiritual motivation we need to make healthy choices. And Dr. Chilton focused on the *how-to*—the nuts and bolts of how to make healthy choices and lose weight. Viewers loved the additional inspiration and the practical information—and it was making a big difference in their lives. Again, they asked for more! In response, we built on the foundation of the web casts to create the *Made to Crave Action Plan*.

Dr. Chilton is a research scientist and nutrition expert who's boiled down the latest scientific discoveries about weight loss and healthy eating into five simple choices anyone can make. In each session throughout the curriculum, you'll learn one or two principles you can put into action that week. In addition to providing the research to help you understand why these choices are so important, Dr. Chilton also equips you with practical guidance so you know how to apply these insights to everyday life.

I love that the Bible says the truth shall set you free (John 8:32). That's a spiritual truth, but it can also be physical truth. The goal of the *Made to Crave Action Plan* is not to squeeze you into a rigid food plan or to beat you up about what you're not doing right. Our goal is to encourage and equip you with truth—spiritual and physical—so you can learn to make better choices. Dr. Chilton's research-based information provides you with truth you can use to help guide your diet to a better place. Do I always pick the healthiest thing? No. But now I know how to arrange my food choices around what is true.

We hope you will experience this curriculum as a grace place, not a legalistic assessment that determines whether you—or anyone else—is "in" or "out." Making one healthy choice is better than being overwhelmed with five and making no healthy choices. And today is a perfect day to start making progress. You don't have to wait until you get your taste buds all cleaned up. If you wait for the perfect day to start a healthy eating plan, that perfect day just never comes—I know that from personal experience. It's time to get unstuck; it's time to start making progress. And the good news is that it's possible— with God's help, you *can* do this. I know that from personal experience too.

Dr. Chilton and I would love to stay connected with you throughout your *Made to Crave* journey. Be sure to visit *MadetoCrave.org* and *GeneSmart.com*, where you'll find many additional resources. We can also connect on my blog, *www.LysaTerKeurst.com*. Please stop by and post a comment or two. I'd love to know how you're doing and continue walking with you even after the study is done.

My dear friend, are you ready to take your first step on this amazing spiritual journey? I promise God will meet you there—and Dr. Chilton and I will be cheering you on every step of the way.

Lysa

How to Use This Guide

Group Size

The *Made to Crave Action Plan* video curriculum is designed to be experienced in a group setting such as a Bible study, Sunday school class, or any small group gathering. To ensure everyone has enough time to participate in discussions, it is recommended that large groups break up into smaller groups of four to six people each.

Materials Needed

Each participant should have her own participant's guide, which includes notes for video segments, directions for activities and discussion questions, as well as personal studies and action plans to deepen learning between sessions.

Timing

The time notations—for example (17 minutes)—indicate the *actual* time of video segments and the *suggested* times for each activity or discussion. For example:

> **Individual Activity:** *What I Want to Remember* (2 MINUTES)

Adhering to the suggested times will enable you to complete each session in one hour. If you have additional time, you may wish to allow more time for discussion and activities.

Facilitation

Each group should appoint a facilitator who is responsible for starting the video and for keeping track of time during discussions and activities. Facilitators may also read questions aloud and monitor discussions, prompting participants to respond and assuring that everyone has the opportunity to participate.

Between-Sessions Personal Studies and Action Plans

Maximize the impact of the course with additional study and action planning between group sessions. Every personal study includes a Bible study, action plan, and guided prayer activity. For each session, you can personalize your plan by choosing action items that work best for you. Some action items are simple and can be done within a day or two; others are more involved and may take additional thought and planning. You'll get the most out of each session by choosing your action items early, ideally within one day of your group session.

Setting aside about one hour for personal study will enable you to complete the between-session studies and action plans by the end of the curriculum. For each session, you may wish to complete the personal study all in one sitting or to spread it out over a few days.

Take Action
Identify Your First Steps

Welcome!

Welcome to Session 1 of the *Made to Crave Action Plan*. You're about to embark on a spiritual adventure with great physical benefits! If this is your first time together as a group, take a moment to introduce yourselves to each other before watching the video. Then let's get started!

Video: *Take Action* (27 MINUTES)

Play the video segment for Session 1. As you watch, use the outline (pages 11 – 14) to follow along or to take notes on anything that stands out to you.

Notes

Made to Crave was about finding your "want-to." *Made to Crave Action Plan* is about finding your "how-to."

Most of us feel underweight spiritually and overweight physically.

Combining the power of scientific research, biblical principles, and loving accountability will help us reach our weight loss goals.

We feel defeated when we bounce back and forth between gaining and losing, feeling deprived and feeling guilty, trying to eat healthy and eating whatever we want.

This is an issue physically, emotionally, and spiritually.

This is a grace place.

> God loves you right where you are.
> You can't use up all your grace with God.

The story of Adam and Eve (Genesis 3)

God is asking us to go to a new place.

> We have a physical indication of a spiritual situation.
> We are spiritually underweight and physically overweight.
> *Made to Crave* is about learning to crave God more than we crave food.

"Seek first his kingdom . . . and all these things will be added [given] to you" (Matthew 6:33 NASB).

The Greek word for "seek" is *zeteo* (dzay-teh´-o). It means to crave.

• • •

Influences that make healthy eating hard for people:

- The marketing efforts of the food industry push us to consume 3,800 calories a day. (Average daily calorie intake to maintain current weight is approximately 2,000 calories—1,800 for women and 2,200 for men.)
- God created us with hunter/gatherer genes that would enable us to survive famine.
- There have been dramatic changes in the packaged food industry, including a significant increase in the use of high-fructose corn syrup and refined oils and the removal of whole grains from the food supply.

The impact of these factors and other changes to our food supply has led to terrible problems:

- Obesity
- Inflammatory diseases
- Damaged self-esteem

It's not your fault. You are not bad, horrible, and lazy.

It's important to look at what is healthy for each individual person. We must individually determine what we need and what our goals are.

Five principles for healthy eating and weight loss

1. Add fish (omega-3s)
2. Increase fiber
3. Exercise
4. Reduce calories
5. Increase nutrient-rich fruits and veggies (polyphenols)

These are scientifically proven strategies we can utilize to lose weight without being hungry and to develop a healthy lifestyle.

Increase fiber

Women: 25 grams of fiber a day
Men: 35 grams of fiber a day

Fiber signals satiety genes that tell you you're full. It allows you to diet without being hungry.

Tip: Drinking 16 ounces of water in the morning can reduce your caloric intake by up to 25 percent for that day.

Optional Video: *Interview with Kathrine Lee* (9 MINUTES)

If your group has more than one hour, consider watching this video featuring an interview with Kathrine Lee. Kathrine describes how she has gained and lost weight, and shares the vital importance of building healthy eating efforts on the right foundation.

Group Discussion (31 MINUTES)

Take a few minutes to talk about what you just watched.

1. What part of the teaching had the most impact on you?

A Grace Place

2. One of the first steps in developing long-term healthy eating habits is choosing a food plan. Which of the following movie titles best describes your response when you hear the words "food plan" or "diet"? Share the reasons for your response.

   ☐ *Psycho*   ☐ *Do the Right Thing*
   ☐ *Leap of Faith*   ☐ *Les Miserables*
   ☐ *Mission Impossible*   ☐ *Saving Grace*
   ☐ *Life Is Beautiful*   ☐ *A Time to Kill*
   ☐ *High Noon*   ☐ *Independence Day*

3. Lysa describes how she felt defeated when she continually bounced between gaining and losing, progress and failure, deprivation and guilt. How have your past efforts to eat healthy or lose weight impacted you—physically, emotionally, and spiritually?

4. On the video, Lysa says, "Many times I felt like I was going to use up all my grace with God. Like God would say, 'Enough! You need to go away.'"

- What thoughts or emotions are you aware of when you consider inviting God into your struggles with food?

- What kind of grace or mercy do you need most from God?

- What would help you to feel safe here—to feel that this group is a "grace place"?

Healthy Eating Factors and Principles

5. Dr. Chilton described several factors that make it difficult for people today to eat healthy. *For example*: hunter/gatherer genes; food industry marketing; increased consumption of high fructose corn syrup and refined oils; and diminished use of whole grains.

- After hearing about all these factors, what was your response to Dr. Chilton's statement, "It's not your fault"?

- How do you think this statement might be misunderstood?

6. Dr. Chilton outlined five principles that are scientifically proven to help us get healthy and lose weight: (1) add fish (omega-3s); (2) increase fiber; (3) exercise; (4) reduce calories; (5) increase nutrient-rich fruits and veggies (polyphenols).

- What is your initial reaction to these principles?

- Which of the principles are you most interested in learning more about and putting into practice? Why?

Optional Partner Activity: *Jumpstart Your Action Plan* (10–12 MINUTES)

If your group has more than one hour, consider using this partner activity as part of your meeting.

Each session of this curriculum includes a personal study and action plan to help you make progress in achieving your healthy eating goals. For each week, you'll have several action plan options to choose from. Some are simple and can be done within a day or two; others are more involved and may take additional thought and planning. Knowing what your options are provides a great jumpstart in taking your next steps.

1. Pair up with one other person.
2. Turn to the Action Items list beginning on page 22. Read the list aloud, taking turns after each item.
3. Place a checkmark next to any action item(s) you'd like to consider. (You can still adjust and finalize your plan during your personal study.)
4. Tell your partner the items you checked. Briefly describe why you think these might be good choices for you.

Individual Activity: *What I Want to Remember* (2 MINUTES)

Complete this activity on your own.

1. Briefly review the outline and any notes you took.
2. In the space below, write down the most significant thing you gained in this session — from the teaching, activities, or discussions.

What I want to remember from this session . . .

Closing Prayer

Close your time together with prayer.

Between-Sessions Personal Study and Action Plan

1. On the video, Lysa says that most of us are underweight spiritually and overweight physically. Which of the phrases below best describes your current spiritual condition?

   ☐ Severely malnourished

   ☐ Moderately malnourished

   ☐ Mildly malnourished

   ☐ Adequately nourished

   ☐ Well nourished

   What factors contribute to your current spiritual condition? *For example*: a consistent practice of spiritual disciplines, or the lack thereof; difficult or beneficial circumstances; emotional setbacks or breakthroughs, etc.

2. Struggles with food can cause problems physically, emotionally, relationally, and spiritually. To get a clearer picture of where you are right now, complete the Starting Point Assessment on pages 24 – 26. Respond to the questions below after completing the assessment.

   Would you say your response totals and assessment descriptions for each section seem true of you? Why or why not?

   Physical . . .

   Emotional . . .

   Relational . . .

Spiritual . . .

3. Wherever you are right now, God's loving invitation is to begin a journey to a new place, a grace place. Lysa describes it as a spiritual journey with great physical benefits. How do you feel about embarking on this journey? Circle the number below that best describes your response.

1	**2**	**3**	**4**	**5**	**6**	**7**	**8**	**9**	**10**
Whoa!				**Slow!**					**Let's go!**
I feel resistant and cautious.				I feel mixed — part of me feels resistant and part of me feels excited.					I feel excited and eager to begin.

What might the number you circled indicate about your need for grace?

What kind of grace do you feel you need to help you take your next steps?

4. Page 22 lists three action plan options to help you take next steps. Some are simple and can be done within a day or two; others are more involved and may take additional thought and planning. All of them focus on helping you to establish your starting point.

   • Take a few moments to review the Action Items list on page 22 and to consider the action(s) you might take. Place a checkmark next to any items you want to consider. If you would like to do something not on the list, write your own ideas in the space provided at the end.

   • Go back and review the items you checked. In the chart on page 20, write down the actions you want to take. For each item you list, write down a timeframe in which you will either complete or begin to take that action (*for example*: by Tuesday or within two days, etc.).

After completing your action plan, use the guided prayer on page 21 or your own prayer to conclude your personal study.

MY ACTION PLAN

ACTIONS I WILL TAKE	TIMEFRAME

Guided Prayer

God,

Thank You for inviting me to begin a journey to a new place, a grace place, in my struggles with food.

I feel all kinds of things right now, but I especially feel ...

I am deeply aware of my need for Your grace, specifically for ...

I commit my action plan for this week to You. I ask for Your power and encouragement to achieve my goals. Specifically, I ask for help with ...

Thank You, Lord, for all the grace You've given me my whole life long. Help me to believe deep down in my heart that Your grace will continue to sustain me on this new journey. Amen.

Action Items

☐ **Document your "before."** Use a cloth measuring tape and the worksheet on page 27 to document your current measurements. Ask a friend to measure you. You'll get the most accurate measurements if you allow someone to help you rather than trying to do it yourself. Then, if you'd like, ask your friend to take your "before" picture.

    If you resist the idea of documenting your starting measurements or taking a picture because you think it will be discouraging, try to think of it instead as an investment in future encouragement. Facts are your friends — even if they initially have hard things to say. Documenting your starting point is one of the best ways to mark and celebrate your progress.

☐ **Make an appointment.** Call your doctor and make an appointment for a routine physical. (You knew this one was coming, right?) Weight and inches are helpful indicators of weight loss but they don't provide a complete picture of your health. In order to track progress toward a healthier lifestyle, it's vitally important to include some measurements that only your doctor can provide. It's also essential to get your doctor's input and clearance before starting any new food and exercise plan. Read the guidelines on page 28 before scheduling your appointment.

☐ **Be a food photojournalist for a day (or more).** Get a one-day snapshot of what you typically eat by keeping a food diary and/or by taking pictures. Use a pad of paper or the food diary on pages 30 – 31 to write down what you eat; use your phone or digital camera to take pictures of what you eat. Nothing is too small — gum, two M&M's, half a glass of juice, etc. If it's going into your mouth, write it down and take a picture of it. To get an even clearer snapshot of what you typically eat, consider keeping a food diary and taking pictures for at least three days. (It's okay to make a few photocopies of the food diary.)

    After completing your food diary and photos, take some time to review them. What stands out to you about what you wrote in your food diary? About your photos? Use a pad of paper or your journal to note your observations and to reflect on any insights they provide about your eating patterns.

My Ideas

☐

☐

☐

Starting Point Assessment

For each of the items listed below, rate the degree to which that statement describes you. Use the following scale:

3 = Completely true of me
2 = Mostly true of me
1 = Somewhat true of me
0 = Not true of me

Section A: *Physical*

_____ I have gained and lost weight several times.

_____ I don't have as much physical energy as I wish I did.

_____ I have health concerns that are weight related.

_____ I sometimes eat in secret or hide food.

_____ My food choices are often high in fat or sugar.

_____ I sometimes skip meals.

_____ I avoid stepping on a scale because I do not want to know my weight.

_____ I eat foods typically considered unhealthy fast food several times a week.

_____ I avoid going to the doctor because of my weight.

_____ The clothes I wore at this time last year are uncomfortably tight or no longer fit.

_____ **Section A Total**

Section B: *Emotional*

_____ I think about food way too much.

_____ I feel embarrassed about my weight or appearance.

_____ The thought of changing how I eat makes me feel sad.

_____ I feel defeated and discouraged about issues related to weight or food.

_____ I say negative things to myself ("You're so fat," "You're ugly," "You're not capable of getting your act together when it comes to food").

_____ I feel guilty or embarrassed about what I eat or the size of my portions.

_____ I think I will always struggle with this issue.

_____ I eat for emotional reasons—for comfort, out of boredom, to relieve stress.

_____ I sometimes feel like food is more powerful than I am.

_____ When it comes to food and weight, I feel like I am trapped in a vicious cycle with no way out.

_____ **Section B Total**

Section C: *Relational*

_____ I avoid doing things with friends if the activity requires physical exertion.

_____ I don't have much confidence when meeting someone new because I am self-conscious about my appearance.

_____ My marriage or dating life has been negatively impacted by my weight or other issues related to food.

_____ I avoid reconnecting with old friends because I don't want them to see how much weight I've gained.

_____ Friends or family have made comments about my weight or other issues related to food.

_____ I avoid dating or being intimate with my spouse because of my weight or other issues related to food.

_____ I feel I would be easier to love if food or weight weren't issues in my life.

_____ My kids or others I am close to sometimes seem embarrassed about my appearance.

_____ I avoid spending time with people who are attractive because I feel so unattractive around them.

_____ I feel my relational life has been significantly impacted by my weight or other issues related to food.

_____ **Section C Total**

Section D: *Spiritual*

_____ I'm not sure this is an issue God cares about.

_____ The Bible hasn't really helped me with this area of my life.

_____ I don't see a connection between what I eat and my relationship with God.

_____ I tend to think of overindulgence in food as the "acceptable sin."

_____ When I need comfort, I turn to food before I turn to God.

_____ Prayer doesn't seem to help me with my food issues.

_____ I'm reluctant to bring this issue to God.

_____ I'm open to God challenging me in any area of life except food and exercise.

_____ I sometimes feel angry or resent God for allowing food to be my issue.

_____ I am embarrassed to ask others to pray for me about my struggles with food.

_____ **Section D Total**

Transfer your four section totals to the spaces indicated below.

Section A: Physical _____

Section B: Emotional _____

Section C: Relational _____

Section D: Spiritual _____

IF YOUR TOTAL FOR A SECTION IS ...	IT'S LIKELY THAT ...
23–30	Issues with food routinely cause significant pain or struggle in this area of your life.
15–22	Issues with food often cause pain or struggle in this area of your life.
8–14	Issues with food occasionally cause pain or struggle in this area of your life.
7 or less	Issues with food rarely cause pain or struggle in this area of your life.

Measurements Worksheet

BIOMETRICS	STARTING POINT ___ DATE	ONE MONTH ___ DATE	TWO MONTHS ___ DATE	THREE MONTHS ___ DATE
HEIGHT				
WEIGHT				
BMI Body Mass Index	Refer to the BMI chart on pages 32–33. Note the BMI number and the designation (normal, overweight, etc.).			
BUST	Measure at the fullest part of your bust, across the nipples; your arms should be down.			
WAIST	Measure at your natural waistline, an inch or two above your belly button.			
HIPS	Measure at the widest point; your legs should be together.			
BICEPS	Left Right Measure at the center point between your shoulder and your elbow.	Left Right	Left Right	Left Right
THIGHS	Left Right Measure at the center point between your inseam and your knee.	Left Right	Left Right	Left Right
CALVES	Left Right Measure at the widest point.	Left Right	Left Right	Left Right

Doctor Appointment Guidelines

Before Your Appointment

When you call to schedule your appointment, ask if it's possible to schedule routine blood work a couple days *prior* to your exam. Scheduling blood work ahead of time enables you to discuss the lab results with your doctor during your appointment.

Ask for the lab tests that will give you the information listed on the chart on page 29. Note that some of these tests are sensitive to food and drink. Plan to do your labs as fasting tests: that means nothing to eat and nothing but water to drink for at least eight hours prior to your appointment. The easiest way to do this is to schedule your lab tests for first thing in the morning.

When you have your lab tests done, ask the nurse or technician to send you a copy of your lab results. Record your lab results in the chart on page 29.

During Your Appointment

During your physical exam, tell your doctor you are beginning a new food and exercise plan. (You may want to take along this participant's guide for reference.) Explain that the plan recommends the following:

- Eating wild-caught salmon and other omega-3 fish and/or taking an omega-3 fish oil supplement
- Eating high-fiber foods, with a goal of consuming 25 grams or more of fiber a day
- Eating five to seven servings a day of nutrient-rich fruits and vegetables and possibly taking a green tea (catechin) supplement
- Vigorous exercise (at 50–85 percent of maximal heart rate), 30 minutes a day, five days a week
- A 10–30 percent reduction in daily calorie intake

Ask your doctor if there are any medical reasons that would inhibit or prevent you from following this plan. Follow up with any other questions you may have about the plan, your lab results, or other health concerns and solicit your doctor's guidance. If you weren't able to complete your labs prior to your appointment, ask your doctor about scheduling them now. Be sure to request that a copy of your lab results be sent to you.

Before leaving the doctor's office, consider making a lab-only appointment for three to six months later. Knowing you'll be taking the labs again is a great motivator to stay on track with your plan. To monitor your progress, document your follow-up lab results on the chart on page 29.

Lab Test Chart

LAB TESTS	REFERENCE RANGE	STARTING POINT ___ DATE	THREE TO SIX MONTHS ___ DATE	SIX MONTHS TO ONE YEAR ___ DATE
TOTAL CHOLESTEROL	125–200 mg/dL			
HDL CHOLESTEROL The so-called "good" cholesterol	Greater than or equal to 46 mg/dL			
LDL CHOLESTEROL The so-called "bad" cholesterol	Less than 130 mg/dL			
TRIGLYCERIDES	Less than 150 mg/dL			
GLUCOSE	65–99 mg/dL			
INSULIN	0.0–24.9 mIU/mL			
HS-CRP High Sensitivity C-Reactive Protein	Low risk: less than 1.0 mg/L			
	Average risk: 1.0–3.0 mg/L			
	High risk: above 3.0 mg/L			
OPTIONAL: OMEGA-3 INDEX This test is currently available only through a home blood testing kit. Visit *GeneSmart.com* for more information.				

Food Diary for _____

Date

TIME, LOCATION, POSITION, AND ACTIVITY What time did you eat? Where were you? What were you doing while eating? *9:15 AM, in the kitchen, standing while making breakfast, etc.*	EMOTIONS What thoughts or feelings were you aware of while eating? *stress, relief, comfort, anxiety, etc.*

FOOD
What and how much did you eat?

1 cup cereal
1 apple
1 fiber bar
turkey sandwich (2 slices whole wheat bread, 3 slices turkey, 1 T mayonnaise, lettuce, tomato)

BODY MASS INDEX TABLE

BMI	NORMAL						OVERWEIGHT					OBESE					
	19	20	21	22	23	24	25	26	27	28	29	30	31	32	33	34	35
Height	Weight (pounds)																
4' 10"	91	96	100	105	110	115	119	124	129	134	138	143	148	153	158	162	167
4' 11"	94	99	104	109	114	119	124	128	133	138	143	148	153	158	163	168	173
5'	97	102	107	112	118	123	128	133	138	143	148	153	158	163	168	174	179
5' 1"	100	106	111	116	122	127	132	137	143	148	153	158	164	169	174	180	185
5' 2"	104	109	115	120	126	131	136	142	147	153	158	164	169	175	180	186	191
5' 3"	107	113	118	124	130	135	141	146	152	158	163	169	175	180	186	191	197
5' 4"	110	116	122	128	134	140	145	151	157	163	169	174	180	186	192	197	204
5' 5"	114	120	126	132	138	144	150	156	162	168	174	180	186	192	198	204	210
5' 6"	118	124	130	136	142	148	155	161	167	173	179	186	192	198	204	210	216
5' 7"	121	127	134	140	146	153	159	166	172	178	185	191	198	204	211	217	223
5' 8"	125	131	138	144	151	158	164	171	177	184	190	197	203	210	216	223	230
5' 9"	128	135	142	149	155	162	169	176	182	189	196	203	209	216	223	230	236
5' 10"	132	139	146	153	160	167	174	181	188	195	202	209	216	222	229	236	243
5' 11"	136	143	150	157	165	172	179	186	193	200	208	215	222	229	236	243	250
6'	140	147	154	162	169	177	184	191	199	206	213	221	228	235	242	250	258
6' 1"	144	151	159	166	174	182	189	197	204	212	219	227	235	242	250	257	265
6' 2"	148	155	163	171	179	186	194	202	210	218	225	233	241	249	256	264	272
6' 3"	152	160	168	176	184	192	200	208	216	224	232	240	248	256	264	272	279
6' 4"	156	164	172	180	189	197	205	213	221	230	238	246	254	263	271	279	287

Source: DHHS/NIH National Heart, Lung and Blood Institute; adapted from Clinical Guidelines on the Identification, Evaluation, and Treatment of Overweight and Obesity in Adults: The Evidence Report.

OBESE Cont.				EXTREMELY OBESE														
36	37	38	39	40	41	42	43	44	45	46	47	48	49	50	51	52	53	54
Weight (pounds)																		
172	177	181	186	191	196	201	205	210	215	220	224	229	234	239	244	248	253	258
178	183	188	193	198	203	208	212	217	222	227	232	237	242	247	252	257	262	267
184	189	194	199	204	209	215	220	225	230	235	240	245	250	255	261	266	271	276
190	195	201	206	211	217	222	227	232	238	243	248	254	259	264	269	275	280	285
196	202	207	213	218	224	229	235	240	246	251	256	262	267	273	278	284	289	295
203	208	214	220	225	231	237	242	248	254	259	265	270	278	282	287	293	299	304
209	215	221	227	232	238	244	250	256	262	267	273	279	285	291	296	302	308	314
216	222	228	234	240	246	252	258	264	270	276	282	288	294	300	306	312	318	324
223	229	235	241	247	253	260	266	272	278	284	291	297	303	309	315	322	328	334
230	236	242	249	255	261	268	274	280	287	293	299	306	312	319	325	331	338	344
236	243	249	256	262	269	276	282	289	295	302	308	315	322	328	335	341	348	354
243	250	257	263	270	277	284	291	297	304	311	318	324	331	338	345	351	358	365
250	257	264	271	278	285	292	299	306	313	320	327	334	341	348	355	362	369	376
257	265	272	279	286	293	301	308	315	322	329	338	343	351	358	365	372	379	386
265	272	279	287	294	302	309	316	324	331	338	346	353	361	368	375	383	390	397
272	280	288	295	302	310	318	325	333	340	348	355	363	371	378	386	393	401	408
280	287	295	303	311	319	326	334	342	350	358	365	373	381	389	396	404	412	420
287	295	303	311	319	327	335	343	351	359	367	375	383	391	399	407	415	423	431
295	304	312	320	328	336	344	353	361	369	377	385	394	402	410	418	426	435	443

Eat Smart
Add Fish and Increase Fiber

Group Discussion: *Checking In* (5 MINUTES)

Welcome to Session 2 of the *Made to Crave Action Plan*. A key part of this healthy eating adventure is sharing your journey with others. Before watching the video, take some time to briefly check in with each other about your experiences since the last session. For example:

- What insights did you discover in the personal study?
- What challenges or victories did you experience with your action plan?
- How have you experienced God working in your life?
- What questions would you like to ask the other members of your group?

Video: *Eat Smart* (26 MINUTES)

Play the video segment for Session 2. As you watch, use the outline (pages 35 – 39) to follow along or to take notes on anything that stands out to you.

Notes

We will always be most victorious when we position ourselves to be in the center of God's will.

Being in the center of God's will is not a matter of what we did or didn't eat today. Being in the center of God's will is to be joyful, prayerful, and thankful (1 Thessalonians 5:16–18).

It's important to focus on God rather than the object of our struggle.

We can choose to be women who are ...

Joyful: Our joy is not in our circumstances but in God being with us in this moment.

Prayerful: We can focus our attention on God and use our struggles as a trigger to pray.

Thankful: Thanksgiving moves the heart of God and enables us to see the hand of God in our lives.

Even when our end goal seems very far away, we can rest in the center of God's will.

• • •

The two most important foods for your plan: fish and fiber.

Fish (omega-3s)
  Wild Alaskan salmon (1,000 mg of EPA and DHA)

Omega-3 fatty acids are fats found primarily in fish and fish oils. They protect against things like heart disease, arthritis, allergies, cognitive loss, depression, diabetes, and aging.

There are three major omega-3s:

  1. ALA (alpha linololenic acid)
  2. EPA (eicosapentaenoic acid)
  3. DHA (docosahexaenoic acid)

Different fish contain dramatically different amounts of omega-3s. Cold water marine fish are the best sources for omega-3s.

  • Salmon
  • Mackerel
  • Cod

Omega-6 fatty acids are essential fatty acids — necessary for health — but can be destructive if we eat too many of them.

PUFA: polyunsaturated fatty acid

Omega-3 = good
Omega-6 = bad

Fiber is the part of a plant that humans are not able to digest.

- It occupies your gut.
- It has no calories by itself.
- It signals satiety genes, which tell you you're full.

Recommended fiber intake

    Women: 25 grams of fiber a day
    Men: 35 grams of fiber a day

Two kinds of fiber

    Soluble (dissolves in water)
    Insoluble (does not dissolve in water)

When you eat a lot of fiber, you must drink water.

Research shows that drinking 16 ounces of water at the start of the day reduces calorie intake during the day by up to 25 percent.

At least 25 – 30 percent of fiber intake should be soluble fiber.

One study showed that women who ate the highest levels of fiber had a 45 percent reduction in their chances of having a heart attack.

For more information, see:

- Know Your Fats (page 43)
- Facts and FAQs about Fish and Omega-3s (pages 43–45)
- Nutrient Facts: Fish (pages 46–47)
- Facts and FAQs about Fiber (pages 48–49)
- Nutrient Facts: Fiber (pages 49–52)

Optional Video: *Interview with Steven Furtick* (18 MINUTES)

If your group has more than one hour, consider watching this interview with Steven Furtick, lead pastor of Elevation Church in Charlotte, North Carolina. Pastor Furtick shares some of his own struggles with food as well as the biblical principles he used to overcome them.

Group Discussion (27 MINUTES)

Take a few minutes to talk about what you just watched.

1. What part of the teaching had the most impact on you?

Position Yourself in the Center of God's Will

2. When it comes to weight loss and healthy eating, there are several ways to define success or victory in achieving our goals. *For example*: reaching a goal weight, fitting into a favorite pair of jeans, feeling more energetic, or lowering cholesterol.

   • How have you defined victory in your previous weight loss and healthy eating efforts? What were the positive and negative aspects of how you defined victory?

   • Lysa describes how we can experience victory now — even when our goal seems very far away — by positioning ourselves in the center of God's will. What concerns you or excites you about allowing your healthy eating efforts to be part of your spiritual journey and your relationship with God?

3. When we decide to get healthy, we can focus so much on food — counting calories, eating the right things, exercising portion control — that we become even more consumed with food than before. Or we can choose to shift our focus from food to God, becoming more consumed with God's truth and craving his will for our lives. According to the apostle Paul, making this choice to be in the center of God's will include three things:

   > Be joyful always; pray continually; give thanks in all circumstances, for this is God's will for you in Christ Jesus. (1 Thessalonians 5:16 – 18 NIV 1984)

   • When you consider the challenges of being on a healthy eating plan, which choice do you think might be hardest for you — the choice to be joyful, prayerful, or thankful? Why?

   • This description of God's will focuses not so much on what God wants us to *do* as it does on what God wants us to *be* — joyful, prayerful, thankful. How do you typically think about what it means to follow God's will? Do you think of it more as something you're supposed to do or as someone you're supposed to be?

• How does this description of God's will encourage you or give you hope in connection with your food struggles?

Add Fish and Increase Fiber

4. We tend to associate eating plans primarily with being deprived—eliminating certain foods and reducing our intake of food overall. Although it is necessary to do these things to be healthy and to lose weight, Dr. Chilton's teaching in this session focuses instead on adding and increasing certain foods rather than eliminating and reducing them. His teaching echoes the philosophy of Hippocrates who said, "Let food be your medicine and medicine be your food."

• How do you respond to the idea that there are some foods (fish and fiber) you actually need to eat more of?

• Which do you think will be most challenging for you—eating the recommended amounts of fish and fiber or eliminating and reducing other foods? Why?

5. Dr. Chilton described some of the many benefits of the omega-3s found in oily fish such as salmon and mackerel. These include protecting against things such as heart disease, arthritis, allergies, cognitive loss, depression, diabetes, and the effects of aging. Which of these benefits provides the strongest motivation for you to make eating more fish part of your healthy eating plan?

6. Fiber is a key component in a healthy food plan. It's what tells us we're full. If we get enough of it—25 grams a day for women and 35 for men—it's possible to lose weight without feeling hungry and to experience some terrific health benefits. How do you imagine not feeling hungry would impact your ability to stick to your healthy eating plan? Would it eliminate most, some, or few of your struggles? Why?

Optional Partner Activity: *Jumpstart Your Action Plan* (12–15 MINUTES)

If your group has more than one hour, consider using this partner activity as part of your meeting.

Get a jumpstart on your action plan this week by identifying your options in advance.

1. Pair up with one other person.
2. Turn to the Action Items list beginning on page 57.
3. On your own, briefly read through the list. Place a checkmark next to any action items you'd like to consider. (You can still adjust and finalize your plan during your personal study.)
4. Tell your partner the items you checked. Briefly describe why you think these might be good choices for you.

Individual Activity: *What I Want to Remember* (2 MINUTES)

Complete this activity on your own.

1. Briefly review the outline and any notes you took.
2. In the space below, write down the most significant thing you gained in this session—from the teaching, activities, or discussions.

   What I want to remember from this session . . .

Closing Prayer

Close your time together with prayer.

Good Stuff to Know

Know Your Fats

There are four different kinds of dietary fat. The so-called "bad" fats are saturated and trans fats. Healthier dietary fats are monounsaturated and polyunsaturated fats.

1. *Saturated fats*: These fats come primarily from animals and are solid at room temperature. They include foods such as full-fat cheese and dairy, shortening, butter, margarine, bacon fat, fatty cuts of meat, poultry skin, and tropical oils (coconut and palm). Saturated fat is associated with raising cholesterol levels as well as increasing the risk for developing cardiovascular disease and type 2 diabetes. *Limit or avoid consumption of this fat.*
2. *Trans fats*: These fats are created in food processing when hydrogen is added to vegetable oil, which makes the fat more solid at room temperature. Foods with typically high levels of trans fats include cookies, crackers, cakes, French fries, and doughnuts. Trans fats have been shown to increase HDL (bad cholesterol) and to lower LDL (good cholesterol), which can increase the risk of cardiovascular disease (heart disease and stroke). *Avoid consumption of this fat.*
3. *Monounsaturated fats (MUFAs)*: These fats come primarily from plant sources and are liquid at room temperature but start to turn solid when refrigerated. Examples of foods with monounsaturated fats include avocados, olives, almonds, peanut butter, olive oil, canola oil, and peanut oil. *Consume these fats in moderation.*
4. *Polyunsaturated fats (PUFAs)*: These fats come from plant and animal sources and are liquid both at room temperature and when refrigerated. There are two primary types of PUFAs — omega-6s and omega-3s. High consumption of omega-6s is associated with causing inflammation and with aggravating chronic diseases. Consumption of omega-3s has been shown to be anti-inflammatory and cardio-protective. Examples of foods with high amounts of omega-6s include most cooking oils — safflower, sesame, corn, sunflower seed — as well as poultry and pork fat and some species of fish (tilapia and catfish). *Limit consumption of omega-6 PUFAs.* Omega-3 polyunsaturated fats are found primarily in fish, such as salmon, mackerel, trout, albacore tuna, fish oils, and flax seed oil. *Consume high amounts (four to six servings a week) of omega-3 fats.*

Facts and FAQs about Fish and Omega-3s

Facts

- Omega-3 fatty acids are fats found primarily in fish and fish oils. Studies have found that they protect against heart disease, arthritis, allergies, cognitive loss, depression, diabetes, and aging.
- There are three primary omega-3 fats in food and supplements:
  (1) ALA (alpha linolenic acid), found in flax seed oil
  (2) EPA (eicosapentaenoic acid), found in fish and fish oil supplements
  (3) DHA (docosahexaenoic acid), found in fish and fish oil supplements
- Omega-6 fatty acids are essential fatty acids — necessary for health — but can be destructive if we eat too many of them. Nearly all of us who live in North America eat far too many omega-6s.

- A healthy diet includes at least 500 mg — and ideally 1,000 mg — of omega-3s a day. Specifically, you should try to get 1,000 mg of EPA and DHA (combined) a day.
- Over the course of a week, eat four to six servings of oily fish and/or take a daily fish oil supplement in order to consistently get the recommended amount of EPA and DHA in your diet.

FAQs

Most healthy eating plans advise staying away from anything oily. Why is oily fish a good thing to eat?
If something is oily, it means it has fat in it. It's important to understand that not all fats are created equal (see "Know Your Fats," page 43). The oil in certain kinds of fish is highly enriched with cardio-protective and anti-inflammatory omega-3 fats. This is the one instance when consuming large amounts of fat is equated to dramatic benefits in health.

Are there risks to eating a lot of fish (omega-3s)?
What most people are concerned about when they ask this question is overexposure to toxic substances such as mercury and PCBs. Many studies have examined the benefit-to-risk ratio of consuming omega-3s (by eating fish or taking supplements) compared to the risk of not consuming omega-3s. In all cases — unless you are pregnant or nursing — the studies found that the benefits dramatically outweigh the risks. To diminish the risk of exposure to mercury or PCBs, eat wild-caught rather than farm-raised fish.

What's the best way to get omega-3s when eating out or traveling?
The easiest way to make sure you get sufficient omega-3s is to take a supplement. If you are looking for omega-3s in food while traveling, farmed Atlantic salmon is always a good choice and typically available on many restaurant menus. Canned Albacore tuna and pink salmon are excellent choices when you're out on a picnic or camping.

What are the best non-fish sources of omega-3s?
A fish oil supplement is the best non-fish source of omega-3. As with any supplement, if you are pregnant, nursing, taking medication, or have other health concerns, consult your doctor prior to taking a fish oil supplement.

How do I know if I need a fish oil supplement?
Unless you're going to eat a serving of oily fish every day, or a lot of oily fish every other day, you probably need a supplement. It's very difficult to eat a Western diet — like we have in North America — and get enough omega-3s from food alone.

What should I look for when choosing a fish oil supplement?
If you want to take 1,000 mg a day of EPA and DHA combined, look for double-concentrated supplements and take one with breakfast and one with dinner. Be sure to read the nutrition facts on the back of the bottle and note the serving size (one or two capsules) and the amount of EPA and DHA in a serving. What it says on the front of the bottle is largely irrelevant. For example, if the front of the label says 1,000 mg, it may still include only 300 grams or less of EPA and DHA, with the remaining 700 mg being

other kinds of fats. Also try to find a supplement that is enteric coated, which aids with digestion, so you don't burp it back up.

If you have no current disease and no family history of inflammatory diseases (such as cardiovascular disease, diabetes, etc.), 500 mg of EPA and DHA a day is sufficient. However, if you do have a disease or a family history of inflammatory disease, it's recommended that you take 1,000 mg or more a day.

Can you get too much fish oil?
The American Heart Association recommends up to 3,000 mg EPA and DHA a day for people with elevated triglyceride levels. Staying within the range of 1,000–3,000 mg a day is considered a safe range for most adults. As with any supplement, if you are pregnant, nursing, taking medication, or have other health concerns, consult your doctor prior to taking a fish oil supplement.

Are flax seeds and flax seed oil good sources of omega-3s?
Yes and no. Flax seeds and flax seed oil contain what are called "short-chain" omega-3s. Only "long-chain" omega-3s have health benefits, so the question is whether or not our bodies can effectively convert the short-chain omega-3s to the beneficial long-chain omega-3s. The majority of people who are of European descent do not have the correct genes to convert the short-chain omega-3s in flax seeds and flax seed oil to long-chain omega-3s. Those who are of African descent are more likely to be able to convert them, but there is still a strong possibility that some can't. That's why long-chain PUFAs found in fish oil are a better choice for everyone. While flax seeds and flax seed oil are good to take, they won't provide the cardio-protective and anti-inflammatory benefits of the long-chain omega-3s for most of us. The primary benefit of flax seed is its high fiber content.

How can I know if I'm eating a good ratio of healthy omega-3s to unhealthy omega-6s?
The only unequivocal way to know your ratio is to have a blood test. Currently, the blood test is available only as an in-home kit through GeneSmart (visit *GeneSmart.com*). The test results include the percentage of omega-3s in your blood as well as the ratio of omega-6s to omega-3s. But you don't need a blood test to know that dramatically increasing omega-3s by eating fish and/or taking supplements will markedly improve your omega-6 to omega-3 ratio.

I know omega-3s prevent future disease, but will they also help me to feel better now?
People who have diseases with a pain component (such as osteoarthritis or rheumatoid arthritis) or a visual component (such as psoriasis or atopic dermatitis) will experience the most obvious improvements, typically within a few months. Within a few months, those with diseases like asthma or allergies are likely to have fewer attacks. Cardiovascular disease is called the silent killer because it typically doesn't have any symptoms, but omega-3s are actively protective against heart disease whether or not you can feel it. In fact, in a recent study that compared fibrates and statins such as Lipitor to omega-3s, omega-3s emerged as dramatically more effective than the drugs in preventing heart disease. If every American consumed sufficient omega-3s, the research indicates we would cut the rate of cardiovascular disease by about 40 percent.

Omega-3s have also been shown to significantly decrease the rate at which we age. A recent five-year study found that those taking the highest doses of omega-3s had a rate of aging 62 percent less than those taking the lowest doses of omega-3s.

Nutrient Facts: Fish

Fish Containing the Highest Levels of Omega-3s*

These fish contain more than 1,000 mg of EPA, DPA, and DHA per 3.5-ounce serving and a very favorable ratio of omega-6s to omega-3s.

FISH†	AMOUNT	OMEGA-3S* (MILLIGRAMS)
Atlantic salmon (farmed)	3.5 ounces	3063
Copper River salmon	3.5 ounces	1950
Pink salmon (canned)	3.5 ounces	1699
Atlantic mackerel	3.5 ounces	1512
Coho salmon	3.5 ounces	1317
Bluefin tuna	3.5 ounces	1298
Albacore tuna (canned in water)	3.5 ounces	1084

Sum of EPA (eicosapentaenoic acid), DPA (docosapentaenoic acid), and DHA (docosahexaenoic acid). It is important to note that the omega-3 content of a given fish can vary depending on where, when, and how it is grown. Totals here are averages.
† Fish are raw unless otherwise indicated.
Sources: Journal of the American Dietetic Association, 108: 1178, 2008; USDA National Nutrient Database.

Fish Containing Moderate Levels of Omega-3s*

These fish contain more than 500 mg of EPA, DPA, and DHA per 3.5-ounce serving and a favorable ratio of omegas-6 to omega-3s.

FISH†	AMOUNT	OMEGA-3S* (MILLIGRAMS)
Trout	3.5 ounces	913
Tuna (canned in water)	3.5 ounces	880
Black bass	3.5 ounces	789
Sockeye salmon	3.5 ounces	757
Sea bass	3.5 ounces	671
Swordfish	3.5 ounces	639
Wild Alaskan salmon (canned)	3.5 ounces	630
Oysters	3.5 ounces	622
Shrimp	3.5 ounces	528

Sum of EPA (eicosapentaenoic acid), DPA (docosapentaenoic acid), and DHA (docosahexaenoic acid). It is important to note that the omega-3 content of a given fish can vary depending on where, when, and how it is grown. Totals here are averages.
† Fish are raw unless otherwise indicated.
Sources: Journal of the American Dietetic Association, 108: 1178, 2008; USDA National Nutrient Database.

Fish Containing Low Levels of Omega-3s*

These fish contain less than 500 mg of EPA, DPA, and DHA per 3.5-ounce serving and a reasonable ratio of omega-6s to omega-3s.

FISH†	AMOUNT	OMEGA-3S* (MILLIGRAMS)
Halibut	3.5 ounces	457
Hake	3.5 ounces	406
Tuna	3.5 ounces	379
Snapper	3.5 ounces	376
Wahoo	3.5 ounces	327
Perch	3.5 ounces	314
Mahi Mahi	3.5 ounces	282
Red Snapper	3.5 ounces	274
Skate	3.5 ounces	268
Grouper	3.5 ounces	257
Flounder	3.5 ounces	245
Sole	3.5 ounces	245
Monkfish	3.5 ounces	205
Haddock	3.5 ounces	204
Corvina	3.5 ounces	197
Cod	3.5 ounces	194
Alaskan King crab	3.5 ounces	130

* Sum of EPA (eicosapentaenoic acid), DPA (docosapentaenoic acid), and DHA (docosahexaenoic acid). It is important to note that the omega-3 content of a given fish can vary depending on where, when, and how it is grown. Totals here are averages.

† Fish are raw unless otherwise indicated.

Sources: Journal of the American Dietetic Association, 108: 1178, 2008; USDA National Nutrient Database.

Fish Containing Little or No Omega-3s*

These fish contain little or no EPA, DPA, and DHA per 3.5-ounce serving and a detrimental ratio of omega-6s to omega-3s.

Not recommended.

FISH†
Catfish (farmed)
Tilapia (farmed)

* Sum of EPA (eicosapentaenoic acid), DPA (docosapentaenoic acid), and DHA (docosahexaenoic acid). It is important to note that the omega-3 content of a given fish can vary depending on where, when, and how it is grown. Totals here are averages.

† Fish are raw unless otherwise indicated.

Sources: Journal of the American Dietetic Association, 108: 1178, 2008; USDA National Nutrient Database.

Facts and FAQs about Fiber

Facts

- Fiber is a key to losing weight without feeling hungry. Fiber signals satiety genes that help us to feel full.
- Many studies show that weight loss can be dramatically accelerated if fiber is increased in the diet. Other studies show that the amount of fiber in a person's diet may be the single most important way to maintain weight loss.
- Women need 25 grams of fiber a day and men need 35 grams of fiber a day.
- There are two kinds of fiber: soluble (dissolves in water) and insoluble (does not dissolve in water).
- Soluble fiber is found in such foods as oat bran, oatmeal, beans, peas, barley, citrus fruits, strawberries, and apples.
- Insoluble fiber is found in such foods as whole wheat breads and cereals, cabbage, beets, carrots, brussels sprouts, and cauliflower.
- At least 25 – 30 percent of the fiber you eat should come from soluble fiber — and more is better. This means that for every 25 grams of fiber you eat, at least 6 – 8 grams should be soluble fiber.

FAQs

What does it mean that fiber has no calories? How is that possible?
Obviously, the foods we eat that have fiber in them do have calories. And, theoretically, fiber would have calories if the human digestive system could absorb it. The reason fiber has no calories is because we don't absorb it. Fiber moves through the gut but it typically does not enter the blood stream, which means we don't derive energy from it in the form of calories.

Is it okay to get some of my fiber in supplements such as capsules or powdered drink mixes (Metamucil, Citrucel, Benefiber, etc.)?
For many reasons, it's ideal to get fiber from whole foods. However, if you find it difficult to routinely get the recommended amount of fiber in your daily diet, a supplement is a good way to help you reach your total. For example, for women, it's okay to get 15 – 20 percent of daily fiber (approximately 4 – 5 grams) from a supplement. There's nothing wrong with supplements as long as you don't depend on them or use them instead of eating nutrient-rich whole foods.

How can I avoid the unpleasant side effects of eating fiber?
Here's the short answer: drink lots of water and eat more soluble fiber.

Insoluble fiber, the kind that doesn't dissolve in water, becomes a hard, solid mass in your gut. It causes gas because it creates air pockets as it moves through your intestines. And it can be painful to pass. Drinking water softens the fiber mass and helps it to move more easily through your digestive system. Soluble fiber, the kind that does dissolve in water, becomes a gel in your gut, which makes it much easier to digest and pass.

To get more soluble fiber into your diet, eat whole foods such as fruits, vegetables, and beans. Try to get at least 25 – 30 percent (6 – 8 grams) or more of your daily fiber from soluble sources.

What's the best way to get enough fiber when eating out or traveling?
Fruits and vegetables are available in most restaurants, even in some fast food restaurants. There are also a wide variety of fiber bars available. Fiber bars are great for when you're away from home because they're easy to take along in a purse, briefcase, or backpack. Keep a few in a drawer at work for those times when you need a quick and healthy snack.

Nutrient Facts: Fiber

Foods Containing High Levels of Fiber Per Serving

These foods contain 7 or more grams of fiber per serving.

FOOD	AMOUNT	FIBER (GRAMS)
Black beans, dried	¼ cup	7.4
Bulgur wheat, quick cooking	¼ cup	7
Cereal, bran	½ cup	10
Cereal, raisin bran	1 cup	7
Cereal, shredded wheat, spoon size	1¼ cup	8
Couscous, whole wheat, dry	⅓ cup	7
English muffin, light, whole grain	1 muffin	8
Flax seeds	3 teaspoons	9
Kidney beans, white, canned	½ cup	10
Great Northern beans, dried	¼ cup	7
Lentils, dried	¼ cup	11
Lima beans, dried	¼ cup	7
Navy beans, dried	¼ cup	9
Pearled barley, dried	¼ cup	8
Pinto beans, canned	½ cup	8
Popcorn, unpopped	¼ cup	7
Raspberries	1 cup	8
Small red beans, dried	¼ cup	13
Small white beans, dried	¼ cup	9
Split peas, green or yellow, dried	¼ cup	9
Refried beans, fat free, canned	½ cup	7

* Fruits and vegetables are raw unless otherwise indicated.
Sources: USDA National Nutrient Database; GeneSmart.com GoGuide.

Foods Containing Moderate Levels of Fiber Per Serving

These foods contain 3 or more grams of fiber per serving.

FOOD	AMOUNT	FIBER (GRAMS)
Almonds	¼ cup	4
Apple (with skin)	1 medium	5
Apricot, dried	5 pieces	3

Artichoke hearts, whole, canned	2 pieces	4
Bagel, whole wheat	1 bagel	5
Banana	1 medium	3.5
Black beans, canned	½ cup	6
Black eyed peas, dried	¼ cup	4
Black eyed peas, canned	½ cup	3
Blueberries	1 cup	4
Broccoli	1½ cup	3.8
Bread, whole grain	1 slice	3
Brussels sprouts	1 cup	3.3
Carrots, canned	½ cup	3
Cereal, bran flakes	¾ cup	5
Cereal, multigrain	1 cup	3
Corn, canned	½ cup	3
Dates, Medjool, dried	2 dates	3
Edamame, frozen	½ cup	5
Fiber snack bar (Kashi)	1 bar	4
Figs, dried	¼ cup	5
Flax seed meal	2 tablespoons	4
Garbanzo beans (chickpeas), canned	½ cup	6
Kidney beans, red, canned	½ cup	6
Kidney beans, red, dried	¼ cup	5
Kiwifruit	2 kiwis	4.4
Lasagna noodles, whole grain, dry	2 ounces	6
Lentil soup, canned	1 cup	5
Lima beans, canned	½ cup	4
Minestrone soup, canned	1 cup	5
Mustard greens, canned	½ cup	4
Oat bran, dry	⅓ cup	6
Oats, steel cut, dry	¼ cup	4
Oats, old fashioned, dry	½ cup	4
Oats, quick cooking, dry	½ cup	4
Orange, navel	1 medium	3
Peas, canned	½ cup	4
Peas, frozen	⅔ cup	4
Peach, dried	3 pieces	3
Pear	1 medium	5.5
Pecans	¼ cup	3
Pinto beans, dried	¼ cup	5

Pistachios	1 ounce	3
Pita bread, whole wheat	1 (1.5 ounces)	4
Plum, dried (prune)	¼ cup	3
Potato, red, with skin	1 medium	3.6
Pumpkin, canned	½ cup	5
Pumpkin seeds	¼ cup	4
Quinoa, dry	¼ cup	3
Sandwich thins, multigrain	1 bun	5
Sesame seeds	¼ cup	4
Spaghetti noodles, whole wheat, dry	2 ounces	5
Spinach, frozen	1 cup	3
Strawberries, sliced	¾ cup	3
Sunflower seeds	¼ cup	3
Sweet potato	1 medium	4
Tortilla, flour, whole wheat	1 10-inch	3
Turkey chili with beans, canned	1 cup	6
Turnip greens, cooked	1 cup	5
Wild rice, dry	¼ cup	3
Yam, cubed	1 cup	6.2

* Fruits and vegetables are raw unless otherwise indicated.
Sources: USDA National Nutrient Database; GeneSmart.com GoGuide.

Foods Containing Low Levels of Fiber Per Serving

These foods contain less than 3 grams of fiber per serving.

FOOD	AMOUNT	FIBER (GRAMS)
Applesauce, unsweetened	½ cup	2
Apricot	3 medium	2
Asparagus	1 cup	2.8
Avocado	¼ cup	2.5
Beets, canned	½ cup	1
Bread, whole wheat	1 slice	2
Cabbage, chopped	1 cup	2.2
Cantaloupe	¾ cup	1.2
Carrot	1 medium	2
Cauliflower	1 cup	2
Celery	1 stalk	0.6
Cranberries, dried	⅓ cup	2.3
Cucumber, with peel	½ cup	0.3
Eggplant	1 cup	2.8
Grapefruit	½ medium	2.5

Green beans	1 cup	2.7
Green beans, canned	½ cup	1.8
Grits, yellow, quick and regular, dry	¼ cup	1.7
Hummus	2 tablespoons	1
Kale	2 cups	2
Mushrooms	1 cup	1.3
Nectarine	1 medium	2.4
Olives, Kalamata	5	1
Onions, chopped	1 cup	2.7
Papaya	1 cup	2.5
Peach	1 medium	2.2
Peanuts	¼ cup	2.3
Peanut butter, crunchy or smooth	2 tablespoons	2
Peach	1 medium	2
Pepper, sweet	½ cup	1.6
Pineapple	¾ cup	1.7
Plum	2 medium	2
Popcorn, popped	1 cup	2
Potato, russet, with skin	1 medium	2.8
Raisins	¼ cup	2
Rice, long-grain brown, dry	¼ cup	1.6
Rice, long-grain white, dry	¼ cup	0.6
Romaine lettuce	2 cups	2
Spinach	3 cups	2
Spinach, canned	½ cup	2
Sugar snap peas	⅔ cup	2
Summer squash, sliced	1 cup	1
Sweet potato, canned	⅔ cup	2
Swiss chard	2 cups	1
Tomato	1 medium	1.5
Tomato juice	8 ounces	2
Tomato paste	2 tablespoons	2
Walnuts	¼ cup	2
Wheat germ, toasted	2 tablespoons	2
Winter squash, cubed	1 cup	1.7
Zucchini, sliced	1 cup	1

* Fruits and vegetables are raw unless otherwise indicated.
Sources: USDA National Nutrient Database; GeneSmart.com GoGuide.

Between-Sessions Personal Study and Action Plan

1. In his first letter to the church at Thessalonica, the apostle Paul writes that God's will for us is to "be joyful always; pray continually; give thanks in all circumstances" (1 Thessalonians 5:16 – 18 NIV 1984). Notice how he emphasizes the importance of these things with words like *always*, *continually*, and *all*. God's will for us is not occasional, intermittent, or sometimes — it's all-encompassing.

   • Use the continuums below to briefly assess your practice of joy, prayer, and giving thanks. Place an X on each continuum to indicate your response.

   ●───●
   I am rarely joyful.   I am always joyful.

   ●───●
   I rarely pray.   I pray continually.

   ●───●
   I rarely give thanks.   I give thanks in all circumstances.

   • Now consider some of your recent experiences. In the last few days or weeks, how have you noticed God at work in your life, helping you to practice joy, prayer, and giving thanks in all circumstances? (If you struggle to identify a recent experience, write down an area of life in which you want God's help to practice joy, prayer, or giving thanks.)

   I experienced God helping me to practice joy . . .

   I experienced God helping me to practice prayer . . .

   I experienced God helping me to practice giving thanks in all circumstances . . .

- What do your continuums and your recent practices of joy, prayer, and giving thanks reveal about your experiences of being in God's will and of not being in God's will?

- How does this understanding impact your view of what it means to be in God's will with your healthy eating efforts?

2. Read the Action Items list on pages 57 – 59 and consider the next step(s) you might take. (Some are simple and can be done within a day or two; others are more involved and may take additional thought and planning.) Place a checkmark next to any items you want to consider. If you would like to do something not on the list, write your own ideas in the space provided at the end.

    Next, go back and review all of the items you checked. In the chart on page 55, write down the two or three actions you want to take. For each item you list, write down a timeframe in which you will complete or begin to take that action (*for example*: by Tuesday or within two days, etc.).

    As you choose your actions, be gracious with yourself. If you are in an especially demanding season of life, don't allow "shoulds" or guilt to drive your choices. Choose reasonable goals that work for you right now, knowing you can always come back and make additional choices later. Choosing actions balanced with healthy amounts of both grace and challenge is a life-giving way to make progress in achieving your goals.

    After completing your action plan, use the guided prayer on page 56 or your own prayer to conclude your personal study.

MY ACTION PLAN

ACTIONS I WILL TAKE	TIMEFRAME

Guided Prayer

God,

My challenges with food and healthy eating are often so hard and discouraging. Sometimes I am afraid that I won't ever be able to overcome this obstacle in my life. But I also believe that the safest place I could ever be is in the center of Your will. And I want that so much.

In the days ahead...
  help me to experience joy in You, especially when ...

  prompt me to pray, especially when ...

  help me to give You thanks in all circumstances, especially when ...

I commit my action plan for this week to You. I ask for Your power and encouragement to achieve my goals. Specifically, I ask for help with ...

Thank You, Lord, for Your faithfulness to me and for loving me closer to You every day. Amen.

▶ Action Items

Prioritize Learning — and Share What You Discover

☐ **Get the facts.** Review "Facts and FAQs about Fish and Omega-3s" (pages 43–45) and "Facts and FAQs about Fiber" (pages 48–49). Then use resources such as your local library or bookstore, the Internet, smart phone apps, health magazines, or healthy eating cookbooks to learn more about fish, omega-3s, or fiber. Write down three to five new facts you learn and share them with the group the next time you meet.

  ☐ *Bonus challenge:* Collaborate with another member of your group to develop a one- to two-page fact sheet about fish, omega-3s, and/or fiber. Distribute the fact sheet to your group.

☐ **Find recipes.** Use resources such as your local library or bookstore, the Internet, smart phone apps, health magazines, or healthy eating cookbooks to find three to five high-fiber recipes you'd like to make. Try to find recipes with at least 2 grams of fiber per serving, and ideally greater than 4 grams. Email links to the recipes or make copies to share with the group the next time you meet.

  ☐ *Bonus challenge:* Prepare one or two of the recipes before your next group meeting. Share your observations with the group.

☐ **Shop and compare bread or cereal.** Create your own spreadsheet or use the worksheets on pages 60–61 to compare the fiber content in bread or cereal at the store where you typically buy your groceries. What are the highest fiber options you can find? Share your findings with the group the next time you meet.

  ☐ *Bonus challenge:* Complete the worksheets for both bread and cereal.

☐ **Shop and compare fish.** Create your own spreadsheet or use the worksheet on page 62 to identify the variety of fish available at the store where you typically buy your groceries. Focus on varieties with high or moderate levels of omega-3 (refer to the charts on pages 46–47). Look for both fresh and frozen fish. Which of the options you identified are most appealing to you? Share your findings with the group the next time you meet.

  ☐ *Bonus challenge:* Visit two or three different stores to shop and compare fish. *For example*: a local chain grocery store, an independent grocery store, a big-box store, a warehouse/club store, or a dedicated seafood market. Photocopy the blank worksheet on page 62 and use a separate worksheet for each store you visit.

Eat (and Drink) Smart

☐ **Start your day with a drink.** Commit to drinking 16 ounces of water first thing in the morning for five days. (Sixteen ounces is two cups in a liquid measuring cup.)

> ☐ *Bonus challenge:* Commit to drinking 16 ounces of water every morning for a month. Make a simple chart to help you keep track of your progress and put it where you'll be sure to see it every morning.

☐ **Strive for 25.** Plan your meals and snacks so that you get 25 grams of fiber (35 grams for men) a day for at least two days this week. Use the fiber charts on pages 49 – 52 as a reference in your meal planning.

> ☐ *Bonus challenge:* Plan your meals and snacks so that you get 25 grams of fiber (35 grams for men) a day for five days this week. You can do it!

☐ **Go all out for fish**. Plan your meals so that you get four to six 4-ounce servings of fish this week. Use the fish charts on pages 46 – 47 as a reference and focus on fish with moderate to high levels of omega-3.

> ☐ *Bonus challenge:* Plan your meals and snacks so that you get 1,000 milligrams of omega-3 (EPA and DHA combined) a day for five days this week. Go for it!

☐ **Have a grand slam day.** Pick one day to focus on all three — water, fiber, and fish. Plan your meals so that you: (1) drink 16 ounces of water first thing in the morning; (2) get 25 grams of fiber (35 grams for men); (3) get 1,000 milligrams of omega-3 (approximately one 4-ounce serving of a high omega-3 fish [see page 46]).

> ☐ *Bonus challenge:* Plan your meals and snacks to focus on water, fiber, and fish for three to five days this week. Wow!

Practice Joy, Prayer, and Thanksgiving

☐ **Keep a one-day joy journal.** At the top of a pad of paper write, "Joy is ..." Keep the pad with you throughout the day and make a list of everything you notice or experience that inspires joy in you. Pay special attention to those times that could be described as "all circumstances," when choosing joy is a little more challenging. Your list might look something like this:

> *Joy is ...*
> 1. *Hot coffee in my favorite mug*
> 2. *Hearing my daughter laugh*
> 3. *Patience when I needed it most*
> 4. *An encouraging email*
> 5. *The courage to say "I'm sorry"*

Write down at least 30 things — 10 in the morning, 10 in the afternoon, 10 in the evening. At the close of the day, present your list to God in prayer. Thank Him for all the joys you experienced that day.

☐ ***Bonus challenge:*** Increase the challenge factor by making a list of 60 things you notice or experience that inspire joy in you — 20 in the morning, 20 in the afternoon, 20 in the evening.

☐ **Pray around the clock.** Set a timer on your watch, computer, or phone at regular intervals as a prompt for prayer. *For example*: every 30 minutes or every hour, etc. In two sentences, briefly thank God for His goodness and ask Him for whatever you need in that moment.

☐ ***Bonus challenge:*** Write your two-sentence prayers in a journal or on a pad of paper and note the time for each (9:15 a.m., 2:15 p.m., etc.). At the close of the day, take 15 minutes to reflect on your prayers. What do you notice about your prayers throughout the day? Offer your observations to God in prayer.

☐ **Pray with pictures.** Use a digital camera or the camera on your phone to capture images that express your joy, prompt your prayer, and inspire your thanksgiving. Print and display the photos where you will see them often — around your work area, on the refrigerator, or as the wallpaper on your computer screen or phone.

☐ ***Bonus challenge:*** Take enough photos to make a brief slideshow on your computer. Share the slide show at your next group meeting.

My Ideas

☐

☐

☐

Bread Shop and Compare Worksheet

BRAND/NAME	PRICE	SERVING SIZE	CALORIES PER SERVING	TOTAL FIBER PER SERVING
Milton's/Healthy Whole Grain Plus	$3.79	1 slice	90	5 grams

Cereal Shop and Compare Worksheet

BRAND/NAME	PRICE	SERVING SIZE	CALORIES PER SERVING	TOTAL FIBER PER SERVING
Trader Joe's/Organic High Fiber O's	$2.49	1 ¼ cup	190	9 grams

Fish Shop and Compare Worksheet

BRAND/NAME	FRESH, FROZEN OR CANNED?	PRICE/ QUANTITY	NUMBER OF SERVINGS/ SERVING SIZE	NOTES
Trident/Alaskan Salmon Burgers	frozen	$17 12 patties	12 patties 4 ounces each	Wild salmon; from whole filets; 1,360 omega-3s per patty

Embrace the Equation
Exercise and Reduce Calories

Group Discussion: *Checking In* (5 MINUTES)

Welcome to Session 3 of the *Made to Crave Action Plan*. A key part of this healthy eating adventure is sharing your journey with others. Before watching the video, take some time to briefly check in with each other about your experiences since the last session. For example:

- What insights did you discover in the personal study?
- What challenges or victories did you experience with your action plan?
- How did the last session impact you or your relationship with God?
- What questions would you like to ask the other members of your group?

Video: *Embrace the Equation* (30 MINUTES)

Play the video segment for Session 3. As you watch, use the outline (pages 63 – 66) to follow along or to take notes on anything that stands out to you.

Notes

Temptation is Satan's invitation to get our needs met his way instead of God's way.

Three areas where Satan tempts us to meet our needs outside the will of God:

1. Physical needs
2. Material needs
3. Significance needs

Biblical examples: Genesis 3 (Eve), Matthew 4 (Jesus), 1 John 2:15 – 16

Satan's name means "one who casts something between two things to cause a separation."

God sends forth His word to heal us (Psalm 107:18 – 20).

● ● ●

We have to understand the "cost" of food — the impact of calories in and calories out. We must ask, "Is it worth it?"

If we take in 100 extra calories a day for a year, we'll gain 10 pounds.

You can't lose weight without exercising.

One study showed that women who exercised at 75 percent of their maximal heart rate five days a week for 16 months but didn't watch their calories actually *gained* an average of three pounds.

If we are exercising, we cannot give ourselves permission to eat whatever we want. If we do, we'll gain weight.

We have to exercise hard.

- Get permission from your doctor first.

- Do it 25 – 30 minutes a day, five days a week. Initial research suggests exercising in intervals of 10 – 15 minutes at a time throughout the day for a total of 30 minutes may be as effective as exercising for 30 minutes straight.

Exercising hard induces a stress response. Research shows this is necessary to experience the health benefits of exercise.

How to estimate maximal heart rate:

Formula: 220 – (your age) = maximal heart rate (beats per minute)
Example: 220 – 40 = 180 *maximal heart rate for a 40-year-old person*

Hard exercise is in the range of 50 – 85 percent of your maximal heart rate. Your maximal heart rate is the highest rate you can safely achieve through exercise stress.

Lazy is a label that does not come from God. God created you to be courageous.

For more information, see:

- How to Take Your Pulse to Determine Your Heart Rate (page 71)
- How to Lose a Pound (page 73)
- Count the Cost (page 73)
- How Many Calories Do You Need? (pages 73 – 74)

Optional Video: *Interview with J. J. and Renee* (11 MINUTES)

If your group has more than one hour, consider watching this video featuring an interview with J. J. and Renee Swope. The Swopes describe how the *Made to Crave* message helped them with more than just food issues, and they also share the positive changes they've experienced in their marriage and family.

Group Discussion (23 MINUTES)

Take a few minutes to talk about what you just watched.

1. What part of the teaching had the most impact on you?

Temptation and Truth

2. We typically think of temptation as a desire for something bad or forbidden. However, hidden behind temptation is often a legitimate human need. The challenge comes in how we choose to meet that need. Lysa describes temptation as Satan's invitation to get our needs met his way instead of God's way.

   • How do you respond to the idea that hidden behind your temptation may be a legitimate human need?

   • Recall a food-related temptation you faced in the last three to five days. How would you describe the legitimate human need behind the temptation? For example, hidden behind a temptation to eat something not on your food plan might be a legitimate need for comfort or reassurance in the midst of a stressful day.

   • For that same food-related temptation, how would you describe God's invitation to you? In other words, how do you imagine God might want to meet the legitimate need behind the temptation?

3. Lysa describes three primary areas where Satan tempts us to meet our needs outside the will of God. These include physical needs, material needs, and needs for significance. Read Matthew 4:1–11 aloud to see how Satan tempted Jesus in these ways.

   • What legitimate human needs—physical, material, significance—do you recognize behind the temptations Jesus faces?

   • For each temptation (Matthew 4:3, 6, 9), Satan offers Jesus an invitation to meet his human needs in a specific way. How might you describe God's invitation to Jesus for each of those same three temptations?

- Every temptation from Satan conceals a lie. Jesus overcomes each lie by quoting God's truth (Matthew 4:4, 7, 10). What lies might be concealed in the temptations you face with food? How might the truths Jesus used — or other truths from Scripture — help you overcome the lies concealed in the food temptations you face?

Calories In and Calories Out

4. If we take in 100 extra calories a day, we'll gain 10 pounds over the course of a year. The reverse is also true — if we burn an extra 100 calories a day, we can lose 10 pounds in a year. When it comes to healthy eating and exercise, do you tend to esteem or diminish the importance of your small choices? Why?

5. Dr. Chilton described the importance of both healthy eating and exercise in the weight loss equation — we have to reduce the calories we take in *and* increase the calories we put out. To maximize the exercise part of the equation, he offered the following guidelines:

   1. Get clearance from your doctor to engage in vigorous exercise.
   2. Exercise 25 – 30 minutes a day (five days a week). Initial research suggests exercising in intervals of 10 – 15 minutes at a time throughout the day for a total of 30 minutes may be as effective as exercising for 30 minutes straight.
   3. While exercising, work out hard enough to reach and maintain 50 – 85 percent of your maximal heart rate.

   - In your own healthy eating efforts, which part of the weight loss equation do you tend to focus on more — reducing the calories you take in (eating less) or increasing the calories you put out (exercising)? Why?

   - Complete one of the following sentences:

     I *do not* intend to visit my doctor and get clearance to exercise because . . .

     I *do* intend to visit my doctor and get clearance to exercise because . . .

- What thoughts or emotions are you aware of when you consider what it might mean to follow through on all three of Dr. Chilton's exercise guidelines?

6. Multiple studies show that there are formulas to estimate your maximal heart rate. Use the formula below to estimate your maximal heart rate and 50–85 percent of your maximal heart rate. (If you prefer to do the calculations later, use the "One-Minute Target Heart Rate Chart" on page 70 to estimate your maximal heart rate and 50–85 percent of your maximal heart rate.)

Example:

220 – _____40_____ = _____180_____ heartbeats per minute
        My age   My maximal heart rate

_____180_____ X .50 = _____90_____ heartbeats per minute
My maximal heart rate   50 percent of my
                      maximal heart rate

_____180_____ X .85 = _____153_____ heartbeats per minute
My maximal heart rate   85 percent of my
                      maximal heart rate

In order to exercise at 50 to 85 percent of my maximal heart rate, I should have _____90_____ to _____153_____ heartbeats per minute.
        50 percent of my   85 percent of my
        maximal heart rate   maximal heart rate

220 – _____ = _____ heartbeats per minute
        My age   My maximal heart rate

_____ X .50 = _____ heartbeats per minute
My maximal heart rate   50 percent of my
                      maximal heart rate

_____ X .85 = _____ heartbeats per minute
My maximal heart rate   85 percent of my
                      maximal heart rate

In order to exercise at 50 to 85 percent of my maximal heart rate, I should have _____ to _____ heartbeats per minute.
        50 percent of my   85 percent of my
        maximal heart rate   maximal heart rate

How does knowing this information about your heart rate impact the way you view your current exercise routine?

ONE-MINUTE TARGET HEART RATE CHART
ESTIMATED BEATS PER MINUTE AT 50–90 PERCENT OF MAXIMAL HEART RATE

AGE	50%	60%	70%	80%	85%	90%	MAXIMAL HEART RATE*
15	102	123	143	164	174	184	205
20	100	120	140	160	170	180	200
25	97	117	136	156	165	175	195
30	95	114	133	152	161	171	190
35	92	111	129	148	157	166	185
40	90	108	126	144	153	162	180
45	87	105	122	138	148	157	175
50	85	102	119	136	144	153	170
55	82	99	115	132	140	148	165
60	80	96	112	128	136	144	160
65	77	93	108	124	131	139	155
70	75	90	105	120	127	135	150
75	72	87	101	116	123	130	145
80	70	84	98	112	119	126	140

* Maximal heart rate is the highest heart rate you can safely achieve through exercise stress.

Optional Group Activity and Discussion:
Practice Taking Your Pulse (8 MINUTES)

If your group has more than one hour, consider using this activity as part of your meeting.

1. Appoint one person to be a timekeeper. The timekeeper needs a watch or clock with a second hand and will keep time for 60 seconds, 30 seconds, and 10 seconds.
2. Read aloud "How to Take Your Pulse to Determine Your Heart Rate" on page 71.
3. Take a few moments to find the pulse on your wrist and then the pulse on your neck. You may need to reposition your fingertips a bit to find your strongest pulse point. Use either the wrist or neck method to complete the rest of the activity.
4. Practice taking your pulse for 60 seconds. Write your total beats (heart rate) below.

My pulse for 60 seconds: _____
My heart rate

5. Practice again by taking your pulse for 30 seconds and then for 10 seconds. Write your number of beats in the spaces provided and complete the equations for each.

My pulse for 30 seconds: _____ x 2 = _____
Number of beats   My heart rate

My pulse for 10 seconds: _____ x 6 = _____
Number of beats   My heart rate

6. Briefly discuss your experience:

- Which method (wrist or neck) worked best for you?
- What concerns you or interests you about incorporating this practice into your exercise routine?

How to Take Your Pulse to Determine Your Heart Rate

Your heart rate is simply the number of times your heart beats in one minute. According to the National Institutes of Health, a normal resting heart rate is between 60 and 100 beats per minute for adults.

Follow these steps to determine your heart rate.

1. Take your pulse by placing two fingers on the artery in your wrist or the artery in your neck:

- *Wrist (radial pulse)*: Place the pads of your index and middle fingers on the inside of your wrist in line with your thumb. Press lightly until you feel a pulse. Do not use your thumb.
- *Neck (carotid pulse)*: Place the pads of your index and middle fingers below the jaw line between your windpipe and the large muscle on the side of your neck. Press lightly until you feel a pulse. Do not use your thumb.

2. While timing yourself with a clock or wristwatch that has a second hand, count the heartbeats you feel. Determine your heart rate (beats per minute) with one of the following methods:

- Count the beats for 60 seconds.
- Count the beats for 30 seconds and multiply by 2.
- Count the beats for 15 seconds and multiply by 4.
- Count the beats for 10 seconds and multiply by 6.

NOTE: When taking your pulse while exercising, you will need to briefly stop your activity while counting your heartbeats.

Optional Partner Activity: *Jumpstart Your Action Plan* (12–15 MINUTES)

If your group has more than one hour, consider using this partner activity as part of your meeting.

Get a jumpstart on your action plan this week by identifying your options in advance.

1. Pair up with one other person.
2. Turn to the Action Items list beginning on page 80.
3. On your own, briefly read through the list. Place a checkmark next to any action items you'd like to consider. (You can still adjust and finalize your plan during your personal study.)
4. Tell your partner the items you checked. Briefly describe why you think these might be good choices for you.

Individual Activity: *What I Want to Remember* (2 MINUTES)

Complete this activity on your own.

1. Briefly review the outline and any notes you took.
2. In the space below, write down the most significant thing you gained in this session — from the teaching, activities, or discussions.

What I want to remember from this session ...

Closing Prayer

Close your time together with prayer.

Good Stuff to Know

How to Lose a Pound

It takes about 3,500 calories to equal one pound of fat. To lose one pound, you need to burn 3,500 calories more than you take in. By cutting 500 calories from your diet each day, you'd lose about one pound a week (500 calories x 7 days = 3,500 calories). By cutting 250 calories from your diet each day, you'd lose about one pound every two weeks (250 calories x 14 days = 3,500 calories).

Exercise along with cutting calories helps boost your weight loss.

Count the Cost

With every unhealthy food choice, we get to count the cost: *Is this worth the cost of the damage I may do to my health and the additional exercise I will have to do to burn the calories?* To see how counting the cost plays out in everyday choices, consider this scenario ...

Marie is short on time and runs by a local fast food restaurant where she orders a healthy grilled chicken sandwich for lunch. She's feeling pretty good about her choice (350 calories) when the young man behind the cash register asks a dangerous question, "Would you like to get the combo deal that comes with fries and a shake?" Marie's healthy choice suddenly seems far less appealing. Plus, she just noticed on the menu board that she can get a strawberry shake. She thinks, *Strawberries are healthy, right? So maybe that's not such a bad choice after all.* But she hasn't really counted the cost.

If Marie opts for the combo, she'll pick up 380 calories and 19 grams of fat from the medium order of fries. The "healthy" strawberry shake will add another 710 calories and 20 grams of fat. In order to burn off the total meal — almost 1,500 calories — Marie would have to run around a track or on a treadmill for two hours. She would also be damaging her health by clogging her arteries and increasing whole body inflammation with the excessive fats and empty calories.

Counting the cost of a food choice means knowing the price you'll have to pay if you eat it. If you were Marie, what would you say? Is the combo worth it?

How Many Calories Do You Need?

The number of calories you need each day is determined by your age, gender, and activity level. The following charts estimate daily calorie needs for women and men to maintain weight.

Estimated Calorie Needs Per Day for Women to Maintain Weight

AGE	ACTIVITY LEVEL		
	SEDENTARY	MODERATELY ACTIVE	ACTIVE
14–18	1,800	2,000	2,400
19–30	1,800–2,000	2,000–2,200	2,400
31–50	1,800	2,000	2,200
51+	1,600	1,800	2,000–2,200

Source: HHS/USDA Dietary Guidelines for Americans (2010).

(cont.)

Estimated Calorie Needs Per Day for Men to Maintain Weight

AGE	ACTIVITY LEVEL		
	SEDENTARY	MODERATELY ACTIVE	ACTIVE
14–18	2,000-2,400	2,400–2,800	2,800–3,200
19–30	2,400–2,600	2,600–2,800	3,000
31–50	2,200–2,400	2,400–2,600	2,800–3,000
51+	2,000–2,200	2,200–2,400	2,400–2,800

Source: HHS/USDA Dietary Guidelines for Americans (2010).

In order to lose weight, you need to burn 10–30 percent more calories than you take in each day. To calculate a target calorie range for weight loss, log on to GeneSmart.com and use the Calorie Calculator. Example A at right demonstrates how the calculator works. It shows that the estimated daily calories for a 41-year-old woman with a low activity level is 1,762.

In order to lose weight at her current low activity level, she needs to reduce her caloric intake to the range of 1,233–1,586 calories a day. But look at the impact on her calorie range if she increases her daily activity and becomes very active (Example B). Her calorie range for weight loss increases to 1,727–2,220 calories a day.

That's the power of embracing the weight loss equation. Increasing daily activity *and* lowering daily calories will efficiently move you toward your desired weight.

EXAMPLE A

Calorie Calculator

Weight(lbs.):	167
Height:	5 4
Age:	41
Sex:	◯ Male ◉ Female
Activity Level:	Low Activity

Calculate

Calories:	1762
10% Reduction:	1586
20% Reduction:	1410
30% Reduction:	1233

EXAMPLE B

Calorie Calculator

Weight(lbs.):	167
Height:	5 4
Age:	41
Sex:	◯ Male ◉ Female
Activity Level:	Very Active

Calculate

Calories:	2466
10% Reduction:	2220
20% Reduction:	1973
30% Reduction:	1727

Between-Sessions Personal Study and Action Plan

1. Sometimes it's hard to beat temptation because it surprises us — we feel vulnerable when it catches us off guard and we're not prepared. Other times temptation is hard to beat because it's so familiar — we have failed to overcome it many times before and feel trapped in a vicious cycle of defeat.

   Use the chart below to list three to five recent food temptations. What word or phrase best describes what triggered each temptation? Was the temptation difficult because it surprised you and caught you off guard, or because it was familiar and failure felt inevitable?

MY RECENT FOOD TEMPTATIONS	WHAT TRIGGERED THE TEMPTATION?	DID THE TEMPTATION FEEL LIKE A SURPRISE OR FEEL FAMILIAR?
Doughnuts in the conference room	Just seeing them!	Surprise — I didn't expect there would be food at the meeting
Birthday cake and ice cream	Wanting to use food to celebrate	Familiar — I didn't want to feel deprived or left out

2. Whatever our temptations — whether familiar or surprising — the promise of Scripture is that we can overcome them when we look beyond our past failures and trust in God's deliverance.

> Forget the former things; do not dwell on the past. See, I am doing a new thing! Now it springs up; do you not perceive it? I am making a way in the wilderness and streams in the wasteland. (Isaiah 43:18 – 19)

> Since [Jesus] himself has gone through suffering and testing, he is able to help us when we are being tested. (Hebrews 2:18 NLT)

> The righteous person faces many troubles, but the Lord comes to the rescue each time. (Psalm 34:19 NLT)

- The promise of the Isaiah passage is that God is always at work — doing a new thing, nurturing growth, making a way — even when we may not perceive it. What new thing do you sense or hope God might be doing in your life through your healthy eating efforts?

- Choose one of the food temptations you wrote on the chart for question 1. Imagine that you are back in that situation facing the same temptation. However, this time, right next to the food is a basket holding a healthy green plant covered with beautiful flowers. The plant represents the new thing God is nurturing in you through your healthy eating efforts. You're invited to choose between the food and the plant. What do you imagine your first thoughts might be?

In what ways, if any, might the presence of the plant change how you experience the temptation?

- All three Scripture passages (page 76) affirm God's desire to provide for us—to make a way in the wilderness, to help us when we are tested, to come to our rescue. How do you respond to these truths? For example, do you struggle to believe them? Believe them but find it difficult to apply them? Believe and rely on them wholeheartedly?

How does the way you respond to these truths impact your response to temptation?

3. Read the Action Items list on pages 80–84 and consider the next step(s) you might take. (Some are simple and can be done within a day or two; others are more involved and may take additional thought and planning.) Place a checkmark next to any items you want to consider. If you would like to do something not on the list, write your own ideas in the space provided at the end.

Next, go back and review all of the items you checked. In the chart on page 78, write down the two or three actions you want to take. For each item you list, write down a timeframe in which you will complete or begin to take that action (*for example*: by Tuesday or within two days, etc.).

As you choose your actions, be gracious with yourself. If you are in an especially demanding season of life, don't allow "shoulds" or guilt to drive your choices. Choose reasonable goals that work for you right now, knowing you can always come back and make additional choices later. Choosing actions balanced with healthy amounts of both grace and challenge is a life-giving way to make progress in achieving your goals.

After completing your action plan, use the guided prayer on page 79 or your own prayer to conclude your personal study.

MY ACTION PLAN

ACTIONS I WILL TAKE	TIMEFRAME

Guided Prayer

God,

Thank You that You are always at work in my life, even when I don't recognize it. I believe You can use everything I face in life — even temptations — to help me become more like You.

I am thankful for Your work in my life this past week, especially for . . .

In the week ahead, I ask You to . . .
meet my needs, specifically for . . .

help me overcome temptation, especially when . . .

I commit my action plan for this week to You. I ask for Your power and encouragement to achieve my goals. Specifically, I ask for help with . . .

Thank You, Lord, for Your presence in my life and for all the ways You protect and provide for me. Amen.

▶ ## Action Items

Prioritize Learning — and Share What You Discover

☐ **Learn from labels.** Adding or subtracting 100 calories a day can have a significant impact over time — 10 pounds gained or lost in a year. To get a better idea of the portion size and calories of the foods you eat, pull out 10 – 12 packaged or canned food items from your pantry, refrigerator, or freezer. Try to choose items you routinely eat in the course of a week. Read the nutrition facts on the packaging to identify the serving size and calories for that food item. Use the worksheet on page 85 to record your findings. Share any insights or discoveries with the group the next time you meet.

☐ *Bonus challenge:* Portion out one serving size for each food item. If possible, use the same size plate or bowl for each item. What do you notice about each portion? Is it bigger or smaller than you thought? Use the worksheet on page 85 to note your observations. Consider taking a photo of each serving or of all the servings together to help you remember the portion size for each item. Place each portion in a small container or food storage bag for ready access throughout the week. Share your observations and/or your photos with the group the next time you meet.

☐ **Research heart rate monitors.** There are two basic kinds of heart rate monitors: chest strap monitors and wrist (or finger touch) monitors.

Chest-strap monitors: Sometimes referred to as wireless monitors, these devices utilize a strap you wear around your chest to transmit your heart rate to a wristwatch-type device that displays the information.

Wrist monitors: Sometimes referred to as finger touch monitors, these devices look like a wristwatch and take your heart rate when you place your finger on the metal ring surrounding the watch face.

Use the Internet to find out more about these two kinds of heart rate monitors. How does each kind work? What features and benefits are unique to each kind? What is the price range for different models? Use the three worksheets on pages 86 – 88 to record your findings. Share what you learn with the group the next time you meet.

☐ *Bonus challenge:* Do your research in person by visiting a sporting goods store. Call ahead to make sure the store carries both kinds of monitors. At the store, tell the salesperson you are not ready to purchase but are in the process of researching heart rate monitors. Ask the salesperson to briefly demonstrate how to use a chest-strap monitor and a wrist (or finger touch) monitor. Try at least two of the monitors yourself by walking briskly around the store and noting the similarities or differences in how each monitor functions. Use the three worksheets on pages 86–88 to record your findings. Share what you learn with the group the next time you meet.

☐ **Identify your healthiest fast food options — in advance.** Even when we're pressed for time, it's possible to make a healthy choice at a fast food restaurant. The key is knowing in advance what the healthy options are. Choose two or three fast food restaurants near your home or workplace where you might typically eat. For example: Subway, McDonalds, Starbucks, Chik-fil-A, Taco Bell, etc. Use the Internet to find and print the nutritional information for the restaurants you choose. For each restaurant, identify the healthiest option you would enjoy for breakfast, lunch, and dinner. Be sure to check the nutritional information for any beverages you might choose as well. Use the worksheet on page 89 to document your choices.

  ☐ *Bonus challenge*: Print your healthiest option choices on a small card. Keep the card in your wallet so you have it for reference the next time you need it.

Embrace the Equation

☐ **Reduce calories.** Do an Internet search using the phrase "reduce 100 calories." Visit four to six web sites to research various ideas for how to reduce 100 calories from your daily food plan. For example: suggestions at *www.prevention.com/100calories/* include ordering a side salad instead of fries with fast food, choosing Canadian bacon instead of sausage, substituting half the oil in a recipe with applesauce when baking. Use the worksheet on page 90 to write down 10 ideas you'd like to try. Place checkmarks next to two or three of the ideas you will try this week.

  ☐ *Bonus challenge*: Make an "Eat This, Not That!" list for your snacks.* Using the worksheet on page 91, list four to six snacks you once ate that are no longer on your food plan or that you must limit. *For example*: a candy bar, Oreos, potato chips. Then identify a healthy option for that snack that you could eat instead. Use the Internet or the nutrition facts on food packaging to identify the calories for both options and the calories you'll save by choosing the healthy option.

---

* Eat This, Not That! is a series of books by David Zinczenko and Matt Goulding that suggest easy food swaps to help you lose weight. These books are great resources to help you make good choices, especially when eating out.

☐ **Begin to exercise.** If you don't yet have an exercise routine, this is a great time to start! (Remember to get clearance from your doctor before starting any new exercise routine.) Use the activity on pages 92–93 to identify exercise options that honor your preferences. Commit to engaging in the activity or activities you choose for at least three days this week. If you haven't exercised in a while, it's okay to start out slow, but try to work up to at least 25–30 minutes of activity each time you exercise. It's also okay to start out with shorter intervals of 10–15 minutes throughout the day as long as you keep your heart rate up and get 25–30 minutes a day.

> ☐ **Bonus challenge:** Invite a friend to be your workout buddy. Exercising with a friend significantly increases the likelihood of sticking with your routine. It also makes the experience more fun.

☐ **Add some variety and take it up a notch.** Over time, your body will adjust to the exercise stress you put it through. As a result, you might experience a plateau that makes your exercise routine less effective. The more in shape you get, the harder you will have to work to induce a stress response.

Cross-training is a way to vary your exercise routine by using several different forms of exercise. For example, you might alternate between walking and cycling for your cardio exercise during the week or add two days of strength training to your routine. Or you might combine running on a treadmill with strength training and stretching in a one-hour workout.

You may also want to consider increasing the intensity and/or duration of your current activity. For example, add a series of one-minute jogging sprints to your 30-minute walk or increase your walk from 30 to 45 minutes.

Using the worksheet on page 94, briefly review the examples of different kinds of exercise. If you can think of additional examples for each kind of exercise, add them in the space provided. Complete the worksheet by writing down your current exercise routine and then two or three options for ways you could add variety and intensity to your current routine. After reviewing your options, circle one option you will try this week.

> ☐ **Bonus challenge:** Sign up for an exercise class that meets once or twice a week for six to eight weeks. Increase the challenge and fun factor by trying a kind of exercise you've never done before.

☐ **Use your heart rate.** Incorporate checking your heart rate into your exercise routine.

    1. Purchase an affordable heart rate monitor (see page 80 for descriptions of the two basic kinds) or take your heart rate by hand periodically while exercising.

    2. If taking your heart rate manually, first read and practice the guidelines described in steps 2–5 of the optional group activity "Practice Taking Your Pulse" on pages 70–71. Note that you will need access to a wristwatch or clock with a second hand while exercising.

    3. Use the worksheet on page 95 to calculate your target heart rate range.

    4. Check your heart rate periodically while exercising. Increase or decrease your activity level to maintain your target heart rate.

  ☐ *Bonus challenge*: Use the worksheet on page 97 to record your heart rate for your exercise routine this week.

  ☐ *Optional challenge*: If taking your heart rate while exercising isn't something you're able or ready to do, use the "Rating of Perceived Exertion Chart" on page 98 to monitor the intensity of your exercise. Work toward achieving between levels 3 and 6, depending on your current fitness level.

Beat Temptation

☐ **Engage in truth training.** Every day this week, start your day by reading through the "Healthy Eating Go-To Scripts" on page 99. Ask God to use these truths to strengthen you and equip you to overcome temptation.

  ☐ *Bonus challenge*: Claim one of the six truths as your focus for each day (it's okay to use the same truth on more than one day). Keep this truth with you by writing it on a card, texting it to your phone, or emailing it to yourself. Read it at least three times throughout the day—perhaps between meals or whenever you are most likely to be tempted to eat something not on your plan. Take the challenge up a notch and commit this truth to memory so you can recite it before you go to sleep that night.

☐ **Talk to your temptations, converse with your cravings.** In an advertising campaign, one weight loss company personified cravings as a little orange monster that chases us around, tempting us to eat unhealthy foods. Use a pad of paper or your journal to reflect on your own experience of cravings and temptation, recently and over time.

  • If you could personify craving based on your experience of it, what form might it take? Would it be like the little orange monster or would it take a different shape? Describe what your craving looks like and how it behaves.

- If you could sit down and have a conversation with this imaginary craving, what do you think it might say to you? What questions would you want to ask it? How do you imagine it might respond?

☐ **Bonus challenge:** Extend the conversation. Set aside 15 – 20 minutes of uninterrupted time to talk with God about your issues related to food. Ask God to join the conversation you've had with your imaginary craving or your temptations. Listen for God's promptings, encouragements, invitations. Ask Him for what you need right now.

☐ **Plant a new thing.** Visit a garden store or nursery and pick out an indoor plant to symbolize the "new thing" God is doing in your life. Print Isaiah 43:18 on a small card and use a ribbon or string to attach it to the pot. Place the plant where you will see it often and use it as a visual cue to help you switch your focus from the object of your temptation to God's new work in you.

☐ **Bonus challenge:** Instead of a green or flowering plant, choose two or three herbs. *For example*: rosemary, parsley, chives, or mint. In addition to using your herb garden as a visual reminder of God's new work in you, enjoy using the herbs to flavor the foods you cook.

My Ideas

☐

☐

☐

Learn from Labels Worksheet

FOOD ITEM	SERVING SIZE	CALORIES PER SERVING	NOTES AND OBSERVATIONS
Kashi TLC Pita Crisps	11 crisps	120	The serving size is larger than I thought!
Sabra Hummus	2 tablespoons	80	Two tablespoons fills half of my small ramekin bowl

Research Heart Rate Monitors Worksheet 1

CHEST-STRAP MONITORS	
How do chest-strap monitors work?	
What are the unique features and benefits of chest-strap monitors?	

WRIST MONITORS *(sometimes referred to as finger touch monitors)*	
How do wrist monitors work?	
What are the unique features and benefits of wrist monitors?	

Research Heart Rate Monitors Worksheet 2

CHEST-STRAP MONITORS		
Brand and Model	Price	Notes and Observations
Omron HR-100C	$59.99	· Includes a chest transmitter belt and a wristwatch-style monitor · Easy to program

Research Heart Rate Monitors Worksheet 3

WRIST MONITORS *(sometimes referred to as finger touch monitors)*		
Brand and Model	Price	Notes and Observations
Timex Health T5K470	*$59.95*	*· Heart rate is displayed in beats per minute and percentage of max heart rate* *· Also tracks calories burned*

Healthiest Fast Food Options Worksheet

RESTAURANT	FOOD ITEM	CALORIES	OTHER NUTRITIONAL INFORMATION THAT'S IMPORTANT TO ME
Chik-fil-A	Chargrilled Chicken Garden Salad	120	· 3.5 grams saturated fat · 4 grams fiber

Reduce 100 Calories Worksheet

TEN OPTIONS I CAN CHOOSE FROM TO REDUCE 100 CALORIES THIS WEEK
☐ 1.
☐ 2.
☐ 3.
☐ 4.
☐ 5.
☐ 6.
☐ 7.
☐ 8.
☐ 9.
☐ 10.

Eat This, Not That! Snacks Worksheet

UNHEALTHY OPTION	UNHEALTHY OPTION CALORIES	HEALTHY OPTION	HEALTHY OPTION CALORIES	CALORIE SAVINGS
Snickers candy bar (2.07 ounces)	280	Kashi's GoLean Crunchy! Protein & Fiber bar	170	110

Exercise Preference Activity

Generally speaking, which item in each of the following statements represents your preference:

a. I prefer to be:
   ☐ Indoors
   ☐ Outdoors

b. I prefer to be:
   ☐ Alone
   ☐ With others

c. I prefer:
   ☐ A quiet environment
   ☐ A lively environment

d. I prefer to learn things:
   ☐ On my own
   ☐ From an instructor

e. I prefer to:
   ☐ Dip my toe in the water
   ☐ Dive in

f. I prefer to be motivated by:
   ☐ One small challenge at a time
   ☐ One big challenge

g. I prefer:
   ☐ A routine
   ☐ Variety

On the chart on page 93 (see example below), use the left column to list the responses you checked for each of the items above. Use the right column to identify two or three forms of exercise or physical activity that honor this preference.

EXAMPLE

MY PREFERENCES	EXERCISE OR PHYSICAL ACTIVITIES THAT HONOR MY PREFERENCES
a. Indoors	· *Walking on a treadmill at the gym* · *Taking an exercise class* · *Working out at home with an exercise video*
b. With others	· *Taking an exercise class* · *Running or walking with a friend* · *Working out with a coach or trainer*
c. Lively environment	· *Listening to music or an audio book on my iPod* · *Taking an exercise class that uses music*

MY PREFERENCES	EXERCISE OR PHYSICAL ACTIVITIES THAT HONOR MY PREFERENCES
a.	
b.	
c.	
d.	
e.	
f.	
g.	

As you review your preferences and the exercise ideas that honor your preferences, what physical activities are the best options for you to try as a starting point?

Cross-Training Ideas Worksheet

TYPE OF EXERCISE	EXAMPLES	MY CURRENT EXERCISE ROUTINE
Cardiovascular	Brisk walking Running Basketball Swimming Kickboxing Cycling Stair climbing Dancing Skating Skiing Rowing Yard work (raking, digging) Racquetball Rope jumping Tennis Step aerobics Water aerobics Other:	Example: Walking 30 minutes three days a week
		OPTIONS I CAN USE TO ADD VARIETY TO MY CURRENT ROUTINE
		Example: Adding strength training with free weights two days a week for 30 minutes
Strength Training	Free weights Core work (push-ups, crunches, pull-ups, etc.) Fitness machines Kettlebells Body bars TRX suspension Resistance (tubes and bands, etc.) Pilates Other:	
		OPTIONS I CAN USE TO INCREASE THE INTENSITY OF MY CURRENT ROUTINE
		Example: Adding four 1-minute jogging sprints during my walk
Flexibility and Balance	BOSU Stability ball Pilates Other:	
Other Exercise Options		

Target Heart Rate Worksheet

1. Use the equations below to estimate your maximal heart rate range and the range for your target heart rate (50–85 percent of your maximal heart rate). If you completed this activity in the group session, transfer your results from page 69.

220 - _____ = _____ heartbeats per minute
        My age   My maximal heart rate

_____ X .50 = _____ heartbeats per minute
My maximal heart rate   50 percent of my
                             maximal heart rate

_____ X .85 = _____ heartbeats per minute
My maximal heart rate   85 percent of my
                             maximal heart rate

In order to exercise at 50 to 85 percent of my maximal heart rate,

I should have _____ to _____ heartbeats per minute.
          50 percent of my   85 percent of my
          maximal heart rate   maximal heart rate

2. If taking your pulse by hand while exercising, you will need to briefly cease your activity to count your heartbeats. As an option, rather than stopping for a full minute (which allows your heart rate to slow down), you can:

    Count your heartbeats for 30 seconds and multiply by 2.

    Count your heartbeats for 15 seconds and multiply by 4.

    Count your heartbeats for 10 seconds and multiply by 6.

If you prefer not to do math while exercising or want a quick assessment, circle or highlight your target heart rate range on the chart on page 96. This will tell you what your target heart rate range should be if you take your pulse for 10 seconds. For example, when taking a pulse for 10 seconds, a woman of 40 should have between 15 and 25 heartbeats in order to be in her target heart rate range while exercising.

TEN-SECOND TARGET HEART RATE CHART

ESTIMATED BEATS PER 10 SECONDS AT 50–90 PERCENT OF MAXIMAL HEART RATE

AGE	50%	60%	70%	80%	85%	90%	MAXIMAL HEART RATE*
15	17	20	24	27	29	31	34
20	17	20	23	27	28	30	33
25	16	19	23	26	27	29	32
30	16	19	22	25	27	28	32
35	15	18	21	25	26	28	31
40	15	18	21	24	25	27	30
45	14	17	20	23	25	26	29
50	14	17	20	23	24	25	28
55	14	16	19	22	23	25	27
60	13	16	19	21	23	24	27
65	13	15	18	21	22	23	26
70	12	15	17	20	21	22	25
75	12	14	17	19	20	22	24
80	11	14	16	19	20	21	23

* Maximal heart rate is the highest heart rate you can safely achieve through exercise stress.

3. If you are taking the bonus challenge, use the worksheet on page 97 to document your heart rate during exercise this week.

Heart Rate Worksheet

DAY	ACTIVITY	DURATION	HEART RATE RIGHT BEFORE EXERCISE	HEART RATE DURING EXERCISE	HEART RATE RIGHT AFTER EXERCISE
Monday	Brisk walking	30 minutes	68	92 / 118 / 124	116

Rating of Perceived Exertion Chart

RATING OF PERCEIVED EXERTION (RPE)		
0	Nothing at all	No change in rate of breathing.
1	Very easy	Mild increase in rate of breathing; able to talk and sing.
2	Easy	
3	Moderate	Noticeable increase in rate of breathing; able to talk but difficult or unable to sing.
4	Somewhat hard	
5	Hard	Noticeable increase in depth and rate of breathing; difficulty talking in complete sentences.
6		
7	Very hard	Gasping slightly for breath; unable to talk.
8		
9		
10	Very, very hard	

Sources: Adapted from the American College of Sports Medicine perceived exertion scale and the Reebok University Effort Scale.

Healthy Eating Go-To Scripts

1. God has given me power over my food choices. I am supposed to consume food, but food is not supposed to consume me.

   But he said to me, "My grace is sufficient for you, for my power is made perfect in weakness...." For when I am weak, then I am strong. *(2 Corinthians 12:9–11)*

2. I was made for more than to be stuck in a vicious cycle of defeat.

   You have circled this mountain long enough. Now turn north. *(Deuteronomy 2:3 NASB)*

3. When I am considering a compromise, I will think past this moment and ask myself, "How will I feel about this choice tomorrow morning? Is it worth the cost of the damage I may do to my health and the additional exercise I will have to do to burn the calories?"

   Do you not know that your bodies are temples of the Holy Spirit, who is in you, whom you have received from God? You are not your own; you were bought at a price. Therefore honor God with your bodies. *(1 Corinthians 6:19–20)*

4. When tempted, I will either remove the temptation or remove myself from the situation.

   If you think you are standing strong, be careful not to fall. The temptations in your life are no different from what others experience. And God is faithful. He will not allow the temptation to be more than you can stand. When you are tempted, he will show you a way out so that you can endure. So, my dear friends, flee. *(1 Corinthians 10:12–14 NLT)*

5. When there is a special event, I can find other ways to celebrate rather than blowing my healthy eating plan.

   See, I have placed before you an open door that no one can shut. *(Revelation 3:8)*

6. I have healthy eating boundaries in place not to restrict me but to define the parameters of my freedom.

   I am using an example from everyday life because of your human limitations. Just as you used to offer yourselves as slaves to impurity and to ever-increasing wickedness, so now offer yourselves as slaves to righteousness leading to holiness. *(Romans 6:19)*

Maximize Key Nutrients
Increase Nutrient-Rich Fruits and Veggies

Group Discussion: *Checking In* (5 MINUTES)

Welcome to Session 4 of the *Made to Crave Action Plan*. A key part of this healthy eating adventure is sharing your journey with others. Before watching the video, take some time to briefly check in with each other about your experiences since the last session. For example:

- What insights did you discover in the personal study?
- What challenges or victories did you experience with your action plan?
- How did the last session impact you or your relationship with God?
- What questions would you like to ask the other members of your group?

Video: *Maximize Key Nutrients* (29 MINUTES)

Play the video segment for Session 4. As you watch, use the outline (pages 101–103) to follow along or to take notes on anything that stands out to you.

Notes

"For our struggle is not against flesh and blood, but against the rulers, against the authorities, against the powers of this dark world and against the spiritual forces of evil in the heavenly realms" (Ephesians 6:12).

Satan wants to separate us from the truth and from God's best.

"In addition to all this, take up the shield of faith, with which you can extinguish *all* the flaming arrows of the evil one" (Ephesians 6:16, emphasis added).

Instead of letting situations bring us down, we can receive the "take me up" attitude.

In the original Greek, the word used for "shield" describes a shield with four corners.

Four corners on Lysa's shield of faith:

1. James 1:2

2. Hebrews 11:6

3. Proverbs 3:5–8

4. Luke 17:11–18

● ● ●

It's not bad to have a treat; just pick treats that don't sabotage your healthy eating plan.

Malnutrition in the United States: A recent study suggests that 72 percent of the calories we eat are not recognized by our ancestral genes. They are empty calories.

According to the World Health Organization (WHO), the United States is number one in health care spending but thirty-seventh in performance. Among the reasons for the gap are the obesity epidemic and malnutrition (empty calories).

Polyphenols (päl-i-fē-nôlz) are the compounds in the skin around grapes and other ripe fruits and vegetables. We need to eat five to seven servings a day of foods containing these compounds.

Catechins (ka-tə-kinz) are powerful health-promoting compounds found in green tea. We should have 250–400 mg of these compounds every day.

Most of us don't get enough omega-3 fatty acids. We need 1,000 mg of EPA and DHA a day. That's two double-concentrated fish oil capsules or about four to six servings of fish a week.

For more information, see:

- Facts and FAQs about Polyphenols (pages 109–110)
- Foods with Polyphenols (page 111)

Optional Video: *Interview with Mary and Melissa* (12 MINUTES)

If your group has more than one hour, consider watching this video featuring an interview with Mary Snyder and Melissa Taylor. Mary and Melissa share about their initial resistance to the *Made to Crave* message and the heart change they experienced when they allowed God into their struggles with food and healthy eating.

Group Discussion (24 MINUTES)

Take a few minutes to talk about what you just watched.

1. What part of the teaching had the most impact on you?

Taking Up the Shield of Faith

2. In every struggle we face, Satan's objective is to cause a separation—from other people, from the truth, from God's best for us.

   • How do you think this happens in struggles with healthy eating? In other words, what kinds of separations do you think Satan typically tries to cause when we are struggling to lose weight or make lifestyle changes?

   • Recall a food-related struggle from the past week. If you think about it in terms of Satan's scheme to cause a separation, what do you imagine Satan might have wanted to separate you from?

3. In his familiar passage about the armor of God, the apostle Paul describes the importance of the shield of faith:

   In addition to all this, take up the shield of faith, with which you can extinguish all the flaming arrows of the evil one. (Ephesians 6:16)

   The Greek word Paul uses for "shield" is *thyreos* (thoo-reh-os). It refers to a large rectangular shield used by Roman soldiers. The shield was curved rather than flat, constructed of wood, and covered with layers of leather. Prior to battle, soldiers soaked their shields in water, which provided added protection against flaming arrows.[*] Although a shield is a defensive weapon, this kind of shield was often used when an army engaged in offensive maneuvers; for example, when laying siege in order to capture an enemy fort or other stronghold.[†]

---

[*] Colin Brown, "War, Soldier, Weapon," *New International Dictionary of New Testament Theology*, vol. 3, Colin Brown, gen. ed. (Grand Rapids: Zondervan, 1978, 1986), 966.

[†] Geoffrey W. Bromiley, "Shield," *The International Standard Bible Encyclopedia*, rev. ed., vol. 4 (Grand Rapids: Eerdmans, 1988), 1040.

- What parallels might you draw between the Roman shield—especially its construction and use—and the shield of faith?

- In military battles, defense is about protection and halting the progress of an enemy. Offense is about advancing, taking new ground, and conquering enemy territory. How would you describe the defensive and offensive aspects of your struggles with food?

4. Roman soldiers often used the kind of shield referenced by the apostle Paul when fighting in formation. Standing closely together, soldiers at the front of a unit held shields before them while soldiers in rows behind held shields to their sides or over their heads. It was a tactic referred to as the "tortoise" formation (*testudo* in Latin) because it provided a protective shell around the soldiers.*

---

* "Testudo formation," *www.wikipedia.com* (accessed 23 July 2011). Artwork by Wenzel Hollar (1607–1677); University of Toronto Wenceslaus Hollar Digital Collection (public domain).

- How does this image of the tortoise formation impact your understanding of what it might mean to take up your shield of faith?

- What insights does it provide about the role of faith in your past or current struggles with food?

Making Better Food Choices

5. Malnutrition occurs when our nutrients are out of balance because we don't get enough of the right types of nutrients. In fact, when we routinely consume too many empty calories — foods high in calories and low in the right types of nutrients — it's possible to be at a healthy weight or even overweight and still experience severe malnutrition. Listed below are just a few examples of foods high in sugar and/or fat but typically low in nutrients our bodies can recognize and use.

Soft drinks	Syrups and jams
Alcohol	French fries and other fast foods
Fruit juices	
Candy	White rice
Cookies	White bread
Doughnuts/pastries	Gravies/sauces
Chips	Margarine/butter
Sugary breakfast cereals	Deep-fat fried foods

- Based on their consumption of empty calorie foods, how would you describe the nutrition levels among the people you know well, such as friends and family? Generally speaking, would you say the people you know are most likely malnourished or well nourished?

- How would you describe your own level of nutrition, currently as well as in the past?

6. Dr. Chilton indicated that there are as many as 5,000 compounds in whole fruits and vegetables that can improve our health. Certain classes of these compounds called polyphenols (päl-i-fē-nôlz) and catechins (ka-tə-kinz) have been shown to be particularly beneficial.

• How do you tend to think about fruits and vegetables? For example, do you enjoy them, avoid them, eat them only because you know you should or because they're lower in calories?

• Polyphenols are compounds found primarily in plants, especially in naturally ripened, dark-skinned fruits and vegetables. Current research suggests they may play a significant role in promoting health and preventing disease. Examples of high polyphenol fruits and vegetables include:

Apples	Celery
Blueberries	Cherry or grape
Blackberries	tomatoes
Cranberries	Eggplant
Mangoes	Garlic
Peaches	Onions
Pears	Red cabbage
Strawberries	Sweet potatoes
Broccoli	

Would you say your consumption of these kinds of foods is currently low, moderate or high? What, if anything, prevents you from eating more of these kinds of fruits and vegetables?

- Based on what you learned about polyphenols and catechins from Dr. Chilton on the video, which of the statements below best expresses where you're at right now? Describe the reasons for your response.

  ☐ For now, I will not try to learn more or to make changes in what I eat.

  ☐ It's unlikely I will try to learn more or to make changes in what I eat.

  ☐ I am interested in learning more, but uncertain about whether or not I will make changes in what I eat.

  ☐ I want to learn more and will likely make changes in what I eat.

  ☐ I am very motivated to learn more and will definitely make changes in what I eat.

Optional Partner Activity: *Jumpstart Your Action Plan* (12–15 MINUTES)

If your group has more than one hour, consider using this partner activity as part of your meeting.

Get a jumpstart on your action plan this week by identifying your options in advance.

1. Pair up with one other person.
2. Turn to the Action Items list beginning on page 118.
3. On your own, briefly read through the list. Place a checkmark next to any action items you'd like to consider. (You can still adjust and finalize your plan during your personal study.)
4. Tell your partner the items you checked. Briefly describe why you think these might be good choices for you.

Individual Activity: *What I Want to Remember* (2 MINUTES)

Complete this activity on your own.

1. Briefly review the outline and any notes you took.
2. In the space below, write down the most significant thing you gained in this session — from the teaching, activities, or discussions.

   What I want to remember from this session . . .

Closing Prayer

Close your time together with prayer.

Good Stuff to Know

Facts and FAQs about Polyphenols

Facts

- Polyphenols are the compounds in the skin around grapes and other ripe fruits and vegetables.
- Eat five to seven servings a day of foods containing these compounds.
- Fruits with high polyphenol levels include apples, apricots, blackberries, blueberries, citrus fruits, plums, grapes, raspberries, strawberries, and cherries.
- Vegetables with high polyphenol levels include broccoli, celery, cherry or grape tomatoes, eggplant, onions, red cabbage, and sweet potatoes.
- Eating polyphenol-rich foods is the best way to consume these key nutrients, but you can also boost your polyphenol intake with a green tea supplement.
- When taking a green tea supplement, look for a supplement with 250–400 mg of catechins per serving.

FAQs

What is the difference between polyphenols and catechins?
Just as an apple is one kind of fruit and a carrot is one kind of vegetable, a catechin is one kind of polyphenol. Polyphenols are a large category of compounds or molecules found in plants. Scientific studies have identified three kinds of especially powerful polyphenols:

- Catechins, found in green tea
- Resveratrol, found in dark-skinned fruit and vegetable skins
- Anthacyanins, found in dark-skinned fruit and vegetable skins

Catechins are a category of polyphenols thought to be responsible for what is referred to as the Asian paradox. The Asian paradox is that many Asian men smoke, but there are lower rates of lung cancer among the Asian population than among the Western population. This is attributed to the high consumption of green tea in the Asian diet. Clinical trials have demonstrated the effectiveness of catechins against several types of cancer as well as their ability to increase energy metabolism, lower body weight, and improve fat mass distribution.

Resveratrol, postulated to be the active ingredient in red wine and the skins of dark fruits and vegetables, is thought to be responsible for the French paradox. The French paradox is that the French diet is high in fatty foods, but there is very little cardiovascular disease among the French. This is attributed to the routine consumption of red wine in the French diet.*

Anthacyanins are polyphenols that give fruits and vegetables their red, purple, or blue color. Although the scientific research is still in early stages, anthacyanins have shown promise in reducing the incidents of inflammatory diseases such as arthritis and

---

*We include the information about the French paradox as part of conveying the research findings. The information is not intended as an endorsement or to encourage the consumption of red wine if that goes against your personal convictions.

proliferative disorders such as cancer. Along with resveratrol, anthacyanins are found in high concentration in dark (purple, blue, red) fruits and vegetables and red wine.

Dark chocolate is one of the richest sources of polyphenols. Cocoa contains a variety of polyphenol classes, perhaps most notably the catechins. Numerous studies, including one published in the *Journal of the American Medical Association* in 2007, have demonstrated that dark chocolate (as opposed to milk chocolate) reduces blood pressure and improves insulin sensitivity.

Do dried, canned, and frozen fruits and vegetables have the same amount of polyphenols as fresh fruit and vegetables?

In order for polyphenols such as resveratrol and anthacyanin to be produced in high quality and quantity, two things must happen: the fruit or vegetable must be stressed in some way, and it must be allowed to ripen naturally.

Polyphenols are natural deterrents for fungal and other infections of plants. When a plant is stressed by natural conditions, it produces more polyphenols to ward off pests. The challenge today is that so many of the fruits and vegetables in our food supply have been overbred. They're bred to be pest resistant and to produce high-yield crops that don't require widespread use of chemical pesticides or fungicides. As a result, many of these fruits and vegetables have lost their ability to produce high quantities of beneficial polyphenols.

Most fruits and vegetables are also harvested before they are fully ripe. This makes it easier to ship them to many places in the world — and to have fresh foods available out of season — but it also prevents the development of beneficial polyphenols.

For these reasons, dried, canned, and frozen fruits and vegetables may sometimes be a more reliable source for polyphenols (especially in winter months) because these fruits and vegetables were typically allowed to ripen naturally. To assure high polyphenol levels in fresh fruits and vegetables, try to get heirloom varieties whenever possible.

What should I look for if I want to take a green tea (catechin) supplement?

Several studies indicate that the amount of catechins varies greatly among different manufacturers of green tea supplements, and even among capsules and/or batches produced by the same manufacturer. Because the dietary supplement industry is not highly regulated, it can be difficult to know for sure the precise dose of catechins you are ingesting with a supplement. However, it is reasonable to assume that roughly 25 – 50 percent of the mg weight in a green tea capsule contains active catechins. For example, if the nutrition facts on the back of the bottle indicate a capsule contains 300 mg of green tea, you can reasonably assume that 75 – 150 mg are catechins. The recommended amount of catechins is between 250 – 400 mg a day, so you would need to take two to three capsules of that particular supplement to get the daily amount.

Foods with Polyphenols

FRUITS WITH HIGH POLYPHENOL LEVELS

Apples without skin (apple butter or applesauce)
Apples with skin, red or green
Apple cider and juice
Apricots
Blackberries
Blueberries
Cherries, sweet or sour
Chokeberries
Cranberries
Currants, black or red
Dates

Elderberries
Gooseberries
Grapes, red or purple
Kiwis
Lemons
Ligonberries
Limes
Mangoes
Marionberries
Nectarines
Oranges (navel oranges, blood oranges; also tangelos, tangerines, etc.)

Peaches
Pears
Plums and prunes (dried plums)
Pomegranates
Quinces
Raspberries
Rhubarb
Raisins
Strawberries

VEGETABLES WITH HIGH POLYPHENOL LEVELS

Artichokes
Broccoli
Celery (especially the hearts)
Cherry or grape tomatoes
Corn
Eggplant (aubergine)
Fennel
Garlic

Greens (kale and turnip)
Kohlrabi
Leeks
Lovage
Onions, red and yellow
Parsnips
Raw spinach
Red cabbage

Rutabagas
Scallions
Shallots
Small, spicy peppers
Sweet potatoes
Watercress

LEGUMES, NUTS, AND SEEDS WITH POLYPHENOLS

Almonds
Cashews
Chick peas
Beans, dried (black, red kidney, pinto, black-eyed peas)
English peas

Fava beans
Flax seeds
Green peas
Hazelnuts
Lentils
Nut butters
Pecans

Peanuts
Pistachios
Pumpkin seeds
Snap beans
Sunflower seeds
Walnuts

ADDITIONAL SOURCES OF POLYPHENOLS

Dark chocolate (at least 60 percent or more cacao)
Red wine
Tea (brewed green, black, or Oolong)
Basil
Capers, red or green

Chives
Cinnamon
Curry
Dill weed
Horseradish
Ketchup
Oregano

Parsley
Rosemary
Sage
Tarragon
Thyme
Vinegar

Source: GeneSmart.com GoGuide.

Between-Sessions Personal Study and Action Plan

1. On the video, Lysa taught that whatever struggle we may face, our real struggle is not ultimately a difficult situation or person but Satan, who wants to separate us from God's best. This is the spiritual reality the apostle Paul describes in his letter to the Ephesians:

> For our struggle is not against flesh and blood, but against the rulers, against the authorities, against the powers of this dark world and against the spiritual forces of evil in the heavenly realms. Therefore put on the full armor of God.... In addition to all this, take up the shield of faith, with which you can extinguish all the flaming arrows of the evil one. *(Ephesians 6:12 – 13, 16)*

In her own struggles, Lysa uses her shield of faith and biblical truths to have a "take-me-up attitude." Instead of allowing the fiery arrows and trials of life to get her down, she uses them as a reminder of what her faith can take her up to. She relies on four key biblical truths — the four corners of her shield of faith — to keep her focus on the higher purpose in her struggles.

- Read through the four passages below and use the space provided to note the higher purpose or spiritual benefit each passage describes.

James 1:2

Hebrews 11:6

Proverbs 3:5 – 8

Luke 17:11 – 18

- How might these truths help you to feel God's protection and encouragement when you are struggling—with issues related to food or in any area of life?

2. Briefly review the descriptions of Roman shields in questions 3 and 4 from the group discussion (pages 104–105). Take a few moments to study the image on page 105, noting anything that stands out to you about the overall scene or any of the details.

   In what ways might the image represent your own internal struggles with healthy eating? In other words, if each part of the picture represented some part of you in your battles with food, how would you describe each part? Write your responses in the space provided and/or on the simplified version of the image on page 114.

EXAMPLE

The soldiers behind the walls . . .

This is the part of me that thinks it's under attack when I even start to consider changing the way I eat. Part of me feels threatened or afraid and doesn't want to make changes. I feel defensive and want to protect myself from more disappointment.

The soldiers behind the walls . . .

The soldiers beneath the shields . . .

The wall itself . . .

The weapons ...

The shields or the tortoise formation ...

Other:

3. Take a moment to reflect on the image again. This time, imagine that Jesus is in the picture with you. Where is He? What do you imagine He might do or say? How do you hope His presence might change the scene?

4. Read the Action Items list on pages 118–121 and consider the next step(s) you might take. (Some are simple and can be done within a day or two; others are more involved and may take additional thought and planning.) Place a checkmark next to any items you want to consider. If you would like to do something not on the list, write your own ideas in the space provided at the end.

    Next, go back and review all of the items you checked. In the chart on page 116, write down the two or three actions you want to take. For each item you list, write down a timeframe in which you will complete or begin to take that action (*for example*: by Tuesday or within two days, etc.).

    As you choose your actions, be gracious with yourself. If you are in an especially demanding season of life, don't allow "shoulds" or guilt to drive your choices. Choose reasonable goals that work for you right now, knowing you can always come back and make additional choices later. Choosing actions balanced with healthy amounts of both grace and challenge is a life-giving way to make progress in achieving your goals.

    After completing your action plan, use the guided prayer on page 117 or your own prayer to conclude your personal study.

MY ACTION PLAN

ACTIONS I WILL TAKE	TIMEFRAME

Guided Prayer

God,

Thank You for being my strong fortress and for giving me a shield of faith that connects me to Your divine power.

I am so grateful for Your protection and deliverance this past week, especially for . . .

In the week ahead, I ask You to strengthen my shield of faith, especially when . . .

I commit my action plan for this week to You. I ask for Your power and encouragement to achieve my goals. Specifically, I ask for help with . . .

Thank You, Lord, for Your goodness to me. I surrender myself to Your protection and care. Amen.

▶ Action Items

Prioritize Learning — and Share What You Discover

☐ **Get the facts.** Review "Facts and FAQs about Polyphenols" (pages 109–110) and "Foods with Polyphenols" (page 111). Then use resources such as your local library or bookstore, the Internet, or health magazines to learn more about polyphenols and catechins. Write down three to five new facts you learn and share them with the group the next time you meet.

  ☐ *Bonus challenge:* Develop a one- to two-page fact sheet about polyphenols and catechins. Distribute the fact sheet to your group.

☐ **Find recipes.** Review "Foods with Polyphenols" (page 111). Then use resources such as your local library or bookstore, the Internet, smart phone apps, health magazines, or healthy eating cookbooks to find three to five recipes that use high-polyphenol fruits or vegetables (without adding significant amounts of additional fat or sugar). If possible, try to find recipes that use more than one kind of polyphenol food. *For example*: a spinach salad garnished with nuts or apples baked with cinnamon and nuts. Email links to the recipes or make copies to share with the group the next time you meet.

  ☐ *Bonus challenge:* Prepare one or two of the recipes before your next group meeting. Share your observations with the group.

☐ **Shop and compare green tea.** Use the worksheet on page 122 to identify the variety of green teas available at the store where you typically buy your groceries. Be sure to consider the various forms of available teas, such as powdered or dried (which you can brew at home), as well as bottled green teas in the beverage aisle.

  ☐ *Bonus challenge:* Purchase two or more varieties of green tea and then do a taste test, either on your own or with friends or family members. As an option, bring the tea to your next group meeting and invite everyone to taste the teas and vote for the one they like best.

☐ **Investigate dark chocolate.** Use resources such as your local library or bookstore, the Internet, health magazines, or healthy eating cookbooks to research the health benefits, nutrients, and nutrition facts about dark chocolate. Use the worksheet on page 123 to record your findings. Share what you learn with the group the next time you meet.

  ☐ *Bonus challenge:* Shop and compare the dark chocolate bars available at the store where you typically buy your groceries. What is the option with the highest percentage of cacao? Use the worksheet on page 124 to record your findings. Share what you learn with the group the next time you meet.

Maximize Key Nutrients

☐ **Eat five to seven servings.** A nutrient-rich diet includes five to seven servings a day of high-polyphenol fruits and vegetables. Plan your meals and snacks so you get five to seven servings a day of these fruits and vegetables for at least two days this week. Use the list of polyphenol-rich foods on page 111 as a reference in your meal planning. (NOTE: Although dark chocolate contains polyphenols, it's not a fruit or a vegetable!)

  ☐ *Bonus challenge:* Plan your meals and snacks so you get five to seven servings a day of high-polyphenol fruits and vegetables for five days this week. Include as much variety as possible and consider trying a fruit or vegetable you don't often eat or have never tried.

☐ **Spice it up.** Many spices contain polyphenols. Review the polyphenal spices at the bottom of the list on page 111. Check your pantry or spice drawer and pull out any of the listed spices you already have. Open each container and smell the spice; if it is a dried herb such as basil or parsley, rub the leaves briefly between your fingers before smelling them. Keep your favorite polyphenol spices out on your kitchen counter this week. As you plan your meals, choose recipes that include these spices or be creative in adding them to any foods you prepare this week.

  ☐ *Bonus challenge:* Buy fresh herbs with polyphenols for at least one meal this week. *For example*: basil for pasta sauce, rosemary for roasted chicken, chopped parsley as a garnish for almost anything!

☐ **Make it tea time.** Pick a day to indulge in green tea. Green tea is made of unfermented tea leaves and contains more polyphenols and catechins than black tea or Oolong tea. In order to get the daily recommended 250 – 400 mg of catechins, you need to drink four or five glasses (32 – 40 ounces). Drink it hot one cup at a time, or brew a larger batch in advance if you prefer to drink it cold. You might drink two to three glasses in the morning and another two glasses in the afternoon. Note that, unless otherwise specified, green tea does contain caffeine. Be sure to choose a decaffeinated option if you're sensitive to caffeine.

  ☐ *Bonus challenge:* Commit to tea time for three to five days this week. If possible, use your tea time to take a brief morning or afternoon break. For 5 – 15 minutes, set aside your tasks (they'll still be there when you get back), and enjoy a few moments of quiet and rest with your tea.

Take Up Your Shield of Faith

☐ **Create your shield.** Pull out a large sheet of paper and your craft supplies — colored markers, pencils, crayons, paint, decorative paper, glue, scissors, etc. Draw a large rectangle to symbolize your shield of faith. In each corner of the shield, write a truth from Scripture that gives you strength and encouragement when you are struggling. Choose from the verses listed below or use any of your favorite verses.

Deuteronomy 3:22	Luke 17:11 – 18
Psalm 7:10	John 13:7
Psalm 121:1 – 2	Philippians 2:13
Proverbs 3:5 – 8	Hebrews 11:6
Ecclesiastes 5:20	James 1:2

Color or decorate the shield in any way you like; you may wish to add designs, images, or other words that remind you of God's protection. Use your shield as an encouragement by placing it where you will see it often. Consider using your digital camera or phone to take a picture of it so you can email it to other members of your group or use it as the wallpaper on your computer or phone.

☐ *Bonus challenge:* Use your shield as part of your time alone with God throughout the week. Incorporate your four verses into your prayers, asking God to use these truths to protect and encourage you throughout that day.

☐ **Learn from the big screen.** Rent *Return of the King*, the third movie in the *Lord of the Rings* trilogy based on the books of J. R. R. Tolkien. Pay particular attention to scenes depicting combat, battle preparations, and defensive or offensive use of shields or other weapons. Use a pad of paper or a journal to briefly write down any quotes, scenes, or observations that stand out to you. Pause the movie if need be, so you don't miss anything! Afterward, use your notes to reflect on any insights the movie provides about the spiritual battles in your own life.

☐ *Bonus challenge:* Make it a movie marathon and watch all three *Lord of the Rings* movies! Do it over one weekend or spread it out over a few weeks. Take notes on all three movies and reflect on the unique insights each one provides about such things as perseverance, overcoming obstacles, and defeating evil.

My Ideas

☐

☐

☐

Shop and Compare Green Tea Worksheet

BRAND/NAME	FORM DRIED, POWDERED, BOTTLED?	PRICE	SERVINGS PER CONTAINER	OTHER INFORMATION THAT'S IMPORTANT TO ME
Lipton/Green Tea Superfruit or Purple Açai and Blueberry	Dried	$2.79	20 tea bags	108 tea flavinoids per serving
Arizona/Green Tea with Ginseng and Honey	Bottled	$1.69	5 (8 oz.)	70 calories per serving

Investigate Dark Chocolate Worksheet

What are the health benefits of dark chocolate?	
What nutrients does dark chocolate contain? *For example*: flavonoids, vitamins, minerals.	
What are the nutrition facts about dark chocolate? *For example*: calories, fats, sugars, fiber, protein.	
When you consider your food plan, healthy eating goals, and what you've learned about dark chocolate, what guidelines would help you to enjoy this treat in a healthy way? *For example*: limitations on portion size, not eating on impulse, etc.	

Dark Chocolate Shop and Compare Worksheet

BRAND AND NAME	PRICE	SERVING SIZE	PERCENTAGE OF CACAO	CALORIES PER SERVING	TOTAL FAT/ SATURATED FAT PER SERVING	OTHER INFORMATION THAT'S IMPORTANT TO ME
Ghirardelli Squares	$5.29	4 squares	60%	210	· 16g total · 10g saturated	Comes in a package of 14 separately wrapped squares rather than one bar

Practice the Five Principles
Keep Working Your Plan

Group Discussion: *Checking In* (5 MINUTES)

Welcome to Session 5 of the *Made to Crave Action Plan*. A key part of this healthy eating adventure is sharing your journey with others. Before watching the video, take some time to briefly check in with each other about your experiences since the last session. For example:

- What insights did you discover in the personal study?
- What challenges or victories did you experience with your action plan?
- How did the last session impact you or your relationship with God?
- What questions would you like to ask the other members of your group?

Video: *Practice the Five Principles* (24 MINUTES)

Play the video segment for Session 5. As you watch, use the outline (pages 125–127) to follow along or to take notes on anything that stands out to you.

Notes

Our goal is not a number on a scale. Our goal is to be at peace — physically, emotionally, and spiritually.

Between every trial and blessing is a path we must walk, and the path is perseverance.

"Consider it pure joy, my brothers [and sisters], whenever you face trials of many kinds, because you know that the testing of your faith develops perseverance. Perseverance must finish its work so that you may be mature and complete, not lacking anything" (James 1:2 – 4).

Perseverance bridges the gap between the trial and the blessing of becoming mature and complete, not lacking anything.

We have to "consider it" because we may not feel it.

We need to stake signposts of joy — joy markers — along our pathway of perseverance.

1. *Protection*: This trial is protecting me from something I cannot see.

2. *Provision*: God is providing something so much better than I could have imagined.

3. *Process*: This trial is part of growing closer to Jesus and becoming more like Him.

● ● ●

It's hard to change habits—but once you do, it's a great lifestyle.

Recap

- Calories in, calories out

    Start your day with 16 ounces of water to reduce your calorie intake that day by 20–25 percent.

- Fiber

    Recommended fiber intake:

    25 grams a day for women

    35 grams a day for men

- Exercise

    You don't exercise to lose weight; you exercise for the health benefits and to lose inches. If you want to mark your progress, measure inches lost rather than pounds lost.

- Omega-3s

- Polyphenols

Optional Video: *Interview with Mandisa* (8 MINUTES)

If your group has more than one hour, consider watching this video featuring an interview with gospel singer Mandisa. Mandisa talks about her very public struggle with weight loss — beginning with negative comments made by judge Simon Cowell on *American Idol* — and the turning points that have helped her to lose over 90 pounds.

Group Discussion (29 MINUTES)

Take a few minutes to talk about what you just watched.

1. What part of the teaching had the most impact on you?

The Path of Perseverance

2. Our goal is not a number on the scale. Instead, our goal is to be at peace — physically, emotionally, and spiritually.

   • What encourages or challenges you about this perspective?

   • In which area — physical, emotional, spiritual — do you want to experience greater peace? Share the reasons for your response.

3. Perseverance is the path we walk between a trial and the blessing of maturity (spiritual completeness) that trial brings. Read aloud the phrases below that describe perseverance.

   A dogged and determined holding on
   Resolute and unyielding commitment
   Maintaining a purpose despite difficulty, obstacles, or discouragement
   Steadfast and continued action over a long period
   Holding fast
   A long obedience in the same direction
   Steady persistence
   Hanging in there
   Unwavering in the face of hardship

Choose the phrase that stands out most to you; then use the phrase in a sentence to describe the perseverance you either have or feel you need right now in your healthy eating journey. *For example:* It's not always easy but I am *holding fast* to my food plan. Or: I am struggling to *maintain my purpose because of difficulties, obstacles, and discouragement.*

4. The apostle James describes the vital necessity of perseverance in helping us to become more like Christ:

> *Consider it pure joy,* my brothers and sisters, whenever you face trials of many kinds, because you know that the testing of your faith produces perseverance. Let perseverance finish its work so that you may be mature and complete, not lacking anything. (James 1:2 – 4, emphasis added)

On the video, Lysa says, "We have to *consider it* because we won't always *feel it.*" When we consider something, we take time to think about it carefully. We concentrate on the issue and weigh the possibilities before taking any course of action.

• Take a moment to recall a food-related struggle you experienced in the last week or few days. Briefly describe the experience.

• In practical terms, what does it mean for you to consider this struggle "pure joy"? Is it something that feels fake and forced, or can you do it authentically? Why?

The Five Principles

5. On the video, Dr. Chilton recaps the five principles of healthy eating and weight loss: (1) add fish (omega-3s); (2) increase fiber; (3) exercise; (4) reduce calories; (5) increase consumption of foods that have super-nutrients (polyphenols), especially dark-skinned fruits and vegetables.

   • Which principles have been the most challenging for you to implement or sustain?

   • Which have been the most beneficial or made the biggest impact?

6. Weight loss is an important benefit of following the five principles, but there are also significant benefits for overall health. *For example*: protection against heart disease, arthritis, allergies, cognitive loss, depression, diabetes, and aging. If you had to name just one, which benefit would you say provides the strongest motivation to persevere with your healthy eating plan? Why?

Optional Partner Activity: *Jumpstart Your Action Plan* (12–15 MINUTES)

If your group has more than one hour, consider using this partner activity as part of your meeting.

Get a jumpstart on your action plan this week by identifying your options in advance.

1. Pair up with one other person.
2. Turn to the Action Items list beginning on page 140.
3. On your own, briefly read through the list. Place a checkmark next to any action items you'd like to consider. (You can still adjust and finalize your plan during your personal study.)
4. Tell your partner the items you checked. Briefly describe why you think these might be good choices for you.

Individual Activity: *What I Want to Remember* (2 MINUTES)

Complete this activity on your own.

1. Briefly review the outline and any notes you took.

2. In the space below, write down the most significant thing you gained in this session—from the teaching, activities, or discussions.

What I want to remember from this session . . .

Closing Prayer

Close your time together with prayer.

Get a Headstart on the Discussion for Session 6

Choosing to live a healthy lifestyle is a lifelong journey, but there is only one session left in your *Made to Crave Action Plan* adventure. As part of the group discussion for Session 6, you'll have an opportunity to talk about what you've learned as well as the challenges and victories you've experienced throughout this curriculum. Between now and your next meeting, take a few moments to review the previous sessions. If you'd like, use the worksheet on pages 132–133 to briefly summarize what you've learned and experienced. Then come to the next meeting prepared to celebrate your progress and God's continued faithfulness for the next steps in your healthy eating journey.

Session 6 Headstart Worksheet

Take a few moments to reflect on what you've learned and experienced throughout the *Made to Crave Action Plan* curriculum. You may want to review notes from the video teaching, what you wrote down for "What I Want to Remember" at the end of each group session, entries for the between-session personal studies, action plans, journal entries, etc. Here are some questions you might consider as part of your review:

- What challenges, defeats, or struggles did I experience related to this session?
- What progress, victories, or breakthroughs did I experience related to this session?
- What was the most important thing I learned in this session?
- How did I experience God's peace or presence with me during this session?
- What are my highlights from the group portion of this session (video teaching or discussions)?
- What are my highlights from the personal studies and action plans for this session?
- What else stands out to me about this session?

Use the space provided to briefly summarize what you've learned and experienced for each session.

Session 1
Take Action: Identify Your First Steps (pages 11–33)

Session 2
Eat Smart: Add Fish and Increase Fiber (pages 35–61)

Session 3

Embrace the Equation: Exercise and Reduce Calories (pages 63 – 99)

Session 4

Maximize Key Nutrients: Increase Nutrient-Rich Fruits and Veggies (pages 101 – 124)

Session 5

Practice the Five Principles: Keep Working Your Plan (pages 125 – 142)

Between-Sessions Personal Study and Action Plan

1. Walking the pathway of perseverance on this healthy eating journey may be challenging, but it doesn't have to be grim. According to the apostle James, no matter what we're facing we can choose joy.

   > Consider it pure joy, my brothers and sisters, whenever you face trials of many kinds, because you know that the testing of your faith produces perseverance. Let perseverance finish its work so that you may be mature and complete, not lacking anything. (*James 1:2–4*)

   For a fresh perspective on this familiar passage, read it again from *The Message*:

   > Consider it a sheer gift, friends, when tests and challenges come at you from all sides. You know that under pressure, your faith-life is forced into the open and shows its true colors. So don't try to get out of anything prematurely. Let it do its work so you become mature and well-developed, not deficient in any way. (*James 1:2–4 MSG*)

   - Take a moment to reflect on your *Made to Crave* journey so far. In what ways would you say your faith life has been "forced into the open" or "show[n] its true colors"?

   - When we persevere, we "don't try to get out of anything prematurely." At this point in the journey, what experiences, challenges, or obstacles have left you feeling most vulnerable to quitting prematurely?

2. Lysa described three joy markers — protection, provision, and process — that help her stay on the path of perseverance.

   - Protection: This trial is protecting me from something I cannot see.

     Lysa's example: *In my mind, skinny equaled healthy. If I could have stayed skinny on a diet of chips and soda, I would have. I would never have acknowledged my body's needs for fiber, healthy fats, protein, and other key nutrients. I would never have pursued healthy choices until I was facing a health crisis. Because my weight issue forced me to learn about healthy eating as well as how to prevent disease, be more active, raise healthy children, and maybe even live longer, it gives me a measure of joy that helps me to persevere.*

How might your struggles with food be protecting you from something you cannot see?

• Provision: God is providing something so much better than I could have imagined.

Lysa's examples: *If I had never struggled with my weight, I would have missed out on experiencing God using this trial in my life to love, help, and encourage other people. I've also discovered a surprising love for healthy foods like strawberries, hummus, snap peas, and many other good choices!*

How has God used your struggles with food to provide something better than you could have imagined? If you find it difficult to think of something, how do you hope God might use this trial in your life for something unexpectedly good?

- Process: This trial is part of growing closer to Jesus and becoming more like him.

Lysa's example: *Through it all I've found a closeness to God that I couldn't have imagined would come out of a struggle with food. I've learned that this healthy eating journey isn't as much about losing the weight as it is gaining truth—the truth of who I am in Christ and how I am made for more than this constant, self-defeating struggle.*

In what ways is your healthy eating journey helping you to grow closer to Jesus and to become more like him?

3. For each of the statements below, rate the degree to which it's true of you, using the following scale:

   3 = Completely true of me
   2 = Mostly true of me
   1 = Somewhat true of me
   0 = Not true of me

   _____ I consistently get 1,000 milligrams or more of omega-3 fatty acids (EPA and DHA) a day by eating four to six servings of high-omega-3 fish over the course of a week, or by taking a fish oil supplement twice a day with meals.

   _____ I consistently eat 25 grams or more of fiber each day and try to make sure 30 percent of it is soluble fiber.

   _____ I exercise hard for 30 minutes or more five days a week and monitor my heart rate to maintain exertion at 50–85 percent of my maximal heart rate.

   _____ I consistently make healthy choices to reduce my intake of calories.

   _____ I consistently eat five to seven servings a day of nutrient-rich fruits and vegetables.

   Pick one of the items you rated with the lowest number and circle it. Consider making this principle the focus of your action plan this week.

4. Read the Action Items list on pages 140–142 and consider the next step(s) you might take. (Some are simple and can be done within a day or two; others are more involved and may take additional thought and planning.) Place a checkmark next to any items you want to consider. If you would like to do something not on the list, write your own ideas in the space provided at the end.

 Next, go back and review all of the items you checked. In the chart on page 138, write down the two or three actions you want to take. For each item you list, write down a timeframe in which you will complete or begin to take that action (*for example*: by Tuesday or within two days, etc.).

 As you choose your actions, be gracious with yourself. If you are in an especially demanding season of life, don't allow "shoulds" or guilt to drive your choices. Choose reasonable goals that work for you right now, knowing you can always come back and make additional choices later. Choosing actions balanced with healthy amounts of both grace and challenge is a life-giving way to make progress in achieving your goals.

After completing your action plan, use the guided prayer on page 139 or your own prayer to conclude your personal study.

MY ACTION PLAN

ACTIONS I WILL TAKE	TIMEFRAME

Guided Prayer

God,

Thank You for being with me on this healthy eating journey. I need Your strength and encouragement every day.

I am thankful for all the ways You helped me to persevere this past week, especially for . . .

In the week ahead, please help me to "consider it joy," especially when . . .

I commit my action plan for this week to You. I ask for Your power and encouragement to achieve my goals. Specifically, I ask for help with . . .

Thank You, Lord, for all the ways You protect me, provide for me, and help me to become more like You. Amen.

▶ Action Items

Prioritize Learning — and Share What You Discover

☐ **Keep learning.** Based on the number you rated lowest for question 3 (page 136), check the box below that corresponds to the principle you want to focus on for this week. For example, if you rated the statement about fish and omega-3s the lowest, check that box below.

    ☐ Eat Smart: Add Fish (omega-3s) and Increase Fiber (page 57)

    ☐ Embrace the Equation: Exercise and Reduce Calories (pages 80 – 81)

    ☐ Maximize Key Nutrients: Increase Nutrient-Rich Fruits and Veggies (page 118)

Refer back to the pages indicated for the box you checked. Review the Prioritize Learning action items on those pages and choose one you haven't yet completed (or choose the bonus challenge). Write this activity and the page number on your action plan chart.

Practice the Five Principles

☐ **Keep working your plan.** Based on the number you rated lowest for question 3 (page 136), check the box below that corresponds to the principle you want to focus on for this week.

    ☐ Eat Smart: Add Fish (omega-3s) and Increase Fiber (pages 57 – 59)

    ☐ Embrace the Equation: Exercise and Reduce Calories (pages 80 – 84)

    ☐ Maximize Key Nutrients: Increase Nutrient-Rich Fruits and Veggies (pages 118 – 121)

Refer back to the pages indicated for the box you checked. Review the action items on those pages and choose either an item you have completed but want to repeat or one you haven't yet completed. Write this activity and the page number on your action plan chart.

Practice Perseverance

☐ **Enter the gateway to perseverance.** Use *BibleGateway.com*, the popular online Bible reference tool, to do a word study.

1. Log on to *www.BibleGateway.com*.
2. Click on "Keyword Search."

3. Under "Enter word(s) or phrase(s)," type in the word *perseverance* or *persevere*.

4. Under "Select Versions," click on "search multiple versions." Then use the pull-down menus to select three to five different Bible versions.

5. Scroll down the page and click the button that says, "Search for keyword or phrase."

Print out your results so you have them to refer to later. Then take a few moments to read through the verses online. For any passages that catch your attention, click through to see the context (the verses preceding and following) or to see the entire chapter.

When you are done exploring the web site, use your printout, your Bible, and a pad of paper or your journal to reflect on how these verses connect to your need for perseverance—in your life overall or in your healthy eating journey.

☐ **Collage your joy markers.** Make three collages to symbolize your joy markers—the protection, provision, and process you've experienced on your healthy eating journey.

1. Gather up old magazines, newspapers, catalogs, wrapping paper, greeting cards, empty food cartons, old receipts, whatever! Anything that can be cut up and pasted is fair game. You'll also need scissors, glue, and three pieces of paper (ideally something sturdy such as construction paper or card stock, but any paper will do).

2. Briefly review your joy markers (the answers to question 2 on pages 134–136). Keep these responses in mind as you look through your gathered magazines and other print materials.

3. Cut out any images or words that catch your attention for whatever reason. For now, don't try to make too much sense of what you're choosing; just enjoy the process of looking for words and images that interest you or touch on something related to your responses on pages 134–136). Try to accumulate at least 10–15 words or phrases and at least 20–25 images (depending on the size of your images, you may need more or less).

4. Once you are done clipping, sort your images and your words into three stacks: one for protection, one for provision, and one for process. If you feel you don't have enough words or images for one of the stacks, go back and look for more or create your own words and images using markers or other craft supplies.

5. Briefly review again your joy marker response for protection (page 135). Play with your stack of protection words and images, arranging

them on the paper in any way that pleases you and then attaching them with glue or other adhesive. (It's not necessary to use all of your words and images). Repeat the process for your provision and process collages.

6. Prop up your three collages and take a moment to consider what you see. What thoughts or emotions are you aware of? How do the words and images affirm God's work in you or make you aware of ways you want God to work in you? Talk with God, expressing your gratitude and asking Him for what you need right now.

7. Use your collages as an encouragement by placing them where you will see them often. Consider using your digital camera or phone to take a picture of them so you can email the photo to other members of your group or use it as the wallpaper on your computer or phone.

☐ **Revisit key spiritual practices.** Check the box below next to any spiritual practices you would like to revisit.

☐ Practice Joy, Prayer, and Thanksgiving (pages 58–59)

☐ Beat Temptation (pages 83–84)

☐ Take Up Your Shield of Faith (page 120)

Refer back to the pages indicated for the box you checked. Review the spiritual practice action items on those pages and choose one you haven't yet completed (or choose the bonus challenge). Write this activity and the page number on your action plan chart.

My Ideas

☐

☐

☐

Make a Courageous Choice
Direct Your Heart to Love and Perseverance

Group Discussion: *Checking In* (5 MINUTES)

Welcome to Session 6 of the *Made to Crave Action Plan*. A key part of this healthy eating adventure is sharing your journey with others. Before watching the video, take some time to briefly check in with each other about your experiences since the last session. For example:

- What insights did you discover in the personal study?
- What challenges or victories did you experience with your action plan?
- How did the last session impact you or your relationship with God?
- What questions would you like to ask the other members of your group?

Video: *Make a Courageous Choice* (25 MINUTES)

Play the video segment for Session 6. As you watch, use the outline (pages 143–144) to follow along or to take notes on anything that stands out to you.

Notes

Food is not our enemy. Satan is our enemy.

Your victory is determined by the very next choice you make. Make it a courageous choice. Make it a choice to persevere.

"May the Lord direct your hearts into *God's love* and *Christ's perseverance*" (2 Thessalonians 3:5, emphasis added).

God's love

- Nothing can separate us from God's love (Romans 8:39).
- Love is patient (2 Corinthians 13:4).
- God's love does not depend on our performance (Romans 5:8).

Christ's perseverance

- Jesus is available to walk with you every step of this journey.
- The same power that raised Jesus from the dead is available to you for any situation, big or small.

Optional Video: *Interview with Art and Lysa* (11 MINUTES)

If your group has more than one hour, consider watching this interview with Art and Lysa TerKeurst as they discuss how they have persevered their own love relationship, including as it relates to Lysa's struggle with weight and her speaking and writing ministry.

Group Discussion (28 MINUTES)

Take a few minutes to talk about what you just watched.

1. What part of the teaching had the most impact on you?

God's Love, Christ's Perseverance

2. The apostle Paul wrote 2 Thessalonians to instruct and encourage believers facing many difficulties, including persecution. As part of his prayer for them, he writes "May the Lord direct your hearts to the *love of God* and to the *perseverance of Christ*" (2 Thessalonians 3:5, emphasis added).

   • In what ways do your struggles with food—or with anything in life— make it difficult for you to believe in or to experience God's love for you?

   • The Greek word Paul uses for the word "direct" is *kateuthyno* (kat-yoo-thoo'-no). It means "to make a straight path and to remove any hindrances." When you are struggling, what hindrances make it difficult for you to focus on or to follow Christ's example of perseverance in your own struggle?

3. Sustaining a healthy lifestyle for the long term requires a commitment to making healthy decisions every day, day after day.

   • When you consider what will be required of you to maintain a long-term commitment, how do you hope God's love and Christ's perseverance will help you?

- What difference would it make in your ability to sustain your commitment if you were to rely on God's love but not follow Christ's example of perseverance? Or to follow Christ's example of perseverance but not rely on God's love?

Celebrating the Journey

4. In Session 5, Lysa taught that our real weight loss goal isn't a number on a scale; our real weight loss goal is to be at peace—physically, emotionally, spiritually. How did you experience—or fail to experience—peace throughout this curriculum?

5. What was the most difficult challenge you faced during the curriculum?

6. How would you describe the progress you've experienced? Consider emotional, spiritual, and intellectual progress as well as physical progress.

7. What victories or breakthroughs provided encouragement or motivation to keep going?

8. When you think about the changes you've experienced, how would you complete these sentences:

Before this curriculum I . . .

After this curriculum I . . .

Individual Activity: *What I Want to Remember* (2 MINUTES)

Complete this activity on your own.

1. Briefly review the outline and any notes you took.
2. In the space below, write down the most significant thing you gained in this session—from the teaching, activities, or discussions.

What I want to remember from this session . . .

Closing Prayer

Close your time together with prayer.

As an option, use the blessing on page 148 to mark the end of this study and to close your gathering.

1. The blessing is a responsive reading. Appoint one person to read the lines designated "leader."
2. Allow a moment of silence before reading the blessing. You may wish to close your eyes, inhale deeply, and exhale slowly. Silently ask God to use this blessing to speak to you.
3. Read the blessing responsively to conclude your gathering.

Closing Blessing

Leader: You are fearfully and wonderfully made.
May the God who formed you, body and soul,
continue His transforming work in you.

All: I believe God knows me better than I know myself.
Because my creator loves me, body and soul,
I will trust Him with my whole self.

Leader: May the Lord Jesus Christ, who is our peace,
keep you in perfect peace —
in all places, at all times, in all ways.

All: I believe the Lord Jesus Christ is more powerful
than any trial I face.
Because my Savior understands me, body and soul,
I will trust Him with my whole self.

Leader: May the Holy Spirit, who intercedes on your behalf,
ground you in truth and fill you with joy —
leading you closer each day to the heart of God.

All: I believe the Holy Spirit knows what I need.
Because my Comforter lives in me, body and soul,
I will trust Him with my whole self.

Leader: May God the Father bless us,
may Christ protect us,
the Holy Spirit lead us, all the days of our lives.

All: Amen.

Final Personal Study and Action Plan

1. The verses below highlight three truths about God's love. Read through the list slowly and, if possible, out loud. As you read each passage, listen for the word or phrase that stands out most to you for any reason. You may wish to read through the list twice or even three times to allow these truths to sink in.

   No power in the sky above or in the earth below—indeed, nothing in all creation will ever be able to separate us from the love of God that is revealed in Christ Jesus our Lord. (*Romans 8:39 NLT*)

   Love is patient, love is kind. (*1 Corinthians 13:4*)

   But God showed how much he loved us by having Christ die for us, even though we were sinful. (*Romans 5:8 CEV*)

   • What word or phrase stands out most to you?

   • Why might this word or phrase be significant for you right now?

2. The meaning of the word *perseverance* is closely connected with two other words—*endurance* and *patience*. As you read through the definitions below, underline any words or phrases that highlight what you need most in order to stay on the journey and achieve your healthy eating goals.

   Perseverance: steady persistence in a course of action, especially in spite of difficulties, obstacles, or discouragement

   Endurance: bearing pain and hardships; the ability or strength to continue, especially despite fatigue, stress, or other adverse conditions

   Patience: bearing provocation, annoyance, misfortune, or pain, without complaint, loss of temper, irritation; willingness to suppress restlessness or annoyance when confronted with delay; quiet, steady perseverance; even-tempered care; diligence

For which of the five principles are you most aware of your need for the kind of perseverance you underlined? (Check all that apply.)

☐ Add fish (omega-3s)

☐ Increase fiber

☐ Exercise

☐ Reduce calories

☐ Increase nutrient-rich fruits and veggies (polyphenols)

3. The book of Hebrews describes how Christ is our model of perseverance.

> And let us run with endurance the race God has set before us. We do this by keeping our eyes on Jesus, the champion who initiates and perfects our faith. Because of the joy awaiting him, he endured the cross, disregarding its shame. Now he is seated in the place of honor beside God's throne. Think of all the hostility he endured from sinful people; then you won't become weary and give up. (Hebrews 12:1b–3 NLT)

For a fresh perspective on this familiar passage, read it again from *The Message*:

> Strip down, start running—and never quit! No extra spiritual fat, no parasitic sins. Keep your eyes on Jesus, who both began and finished this race we're in. Study how he did it. Because he never lost sight of where he was headed—that exhilarating finish in and with God—he could put up with anything along the way: Cross, shame, whatever. And now he's there, in the place of honor, right alongside God. When you find yourselves flagging in your faith, go over that story again, item by item, that long litany of hostility he plowed through. That will shoot adrenaline into your souls! (Hebrews 12:1b–3 MSG)

- Based on these two versions of the passage, what wisdom or insights about perseverance do you gain from Christ's example?

- How might these insights help you to persevere with the principle(s) you checked in question 2?

4. Listed below are summaries of the five principles of healthy eating and weight loss. Briefly review the summaries and then circle the number that best describes the degree to which you are currently practicing that principle.

(1) Add fish (omega-3s).

- A healthy diet includes at least 500 – 1,000 mg of omega-3s a day. Specifically, you need at least 500 – 1,000 mg of EPA and DHA (combined) a day.

- Over the course of a week, eat four to six servings of oily fish and/or take a daily fish oil supplement in order to consistently get the recommended amount of EPA and DHA in your diet.

- If using supplements, take two double-concentrated fish oil capsules a day (one with breakfast and one with dinner).

1   2   3   4   5   6   7   8   9   10

In a typical week, I never consume enough omega-3s.	In a typical week, I sometimes consume enough omega-3s.	In a typical week, I always consume enough omega-3s.

(2) Increase fiber.

- Fiber is the key to losing weight without feeling hungry. Fiber signals satiety genes that help you to feel full.

- Women need 25 grams of fiber a day and men need 35 grams of fiber a day.

- There are two kinds of fiber: soluble (dissolves in water) and insoluble (does not dissolve in water).

- Soluble fiber is found in such foods as oat bran, oatmeal, beans, peas, barley, citrus fruits, strawberries, and apples.

- Insoluble fiber is found in such foods as whole wheat breads and cereals, cabbage, beets, carrots, brussels sprouts, and cauliflower.

- Twenty-five to 30 percent of the fiber you eat should come from soluble fiber. This means that for every 25 grams of fiber you eat, 6 – 8 grams should be soluble fiber — and more is even better.

- Eating fiber-rich food is the best way to consume fiber, but you can also boost your fiber intake with a supplement (such as Metamucil, Citrucel, Benefiber).

1	2	3	4	5	6	7	8	9	10
In a typical week, I never consume enough fiber.				In a typical week, I sometimes consume enough fiber.				In a typical week, I always consume enough fiber.	

(3) Exercise.

- Exercise 25 – 30 minutes a day, five days a week.

- Initial research suggests exercising in intervals of 10 – 15 minutes at a time throughout the day for a total of 30 minutes may be as effective as exercising for 30 minutes straight.

- Exercise hard enough to induce a stress response by maintaining exertion at 50 – 85 percent of your maximal heart rate.

- If you are just beginning to exercise, aim for the lower end of your target heart rate zone (50 percent). Then, gradually increase the intensity of your exercise and build up to the higher end of your heart rate zone (85 percent).

1	2	3	4	5	6	7	8	9	10
In a typical week, I never exercise 30 minutes/day, 5 days/week.				In a typical week, I sometimes exercise 30 minutes/day, 5 days/week.				In a typical week, I always exercise 30 minutes/day, 5 days/week.	

(4) Reduce calories.

- To lose weight, reduce caloric intake by 20 – 30 percent of what is needed to maintain your current weight.

- Focus on the "cost" of food and the impact of calories in and calories out. If you eat just 100 calories more than you need a day, you'll gain 10 pounds over the course of a year.

- When making an unhealthy food choice, consider two things: the cost of the food in terms of how much you will have to exercise to burn off the calories, and the cost of how damaging this food is to your overall health.

1   2   3   4   5   6   7   8   9   10

In a typical week, I never reduce my calorie intake.

In a typical week, I sometimes reduce my calorie intake.

In a typical week, I always reduce my calorie intake.

(5) Increase nutrient-rich fruits and veggies (polyphenols).

- Polyphenols are the compounds in the skin around grapes and other ripe fruits and vegetables.

- Eat five to seven servings a day of foods containing these compounds.

- Fruits with high polyphenol levels include apples, apricots, blackberries, blueberries, citrus fruits, plums, grapes, raspberries, strawberries, and cherries.

- Vegetables with high polyphenol levels include broccoli, celery, cherry or grape tomatoes, eggplant, onions, red cabbage, and sweet potatoes.

- Eating polyphenol-rich foods is the best way to consume these key nutrients, but you can also boost your polyphenol intake with a green tea supplement.

- When taking a green tea supplement, look for a supplement with 250–400 mg of catechins per capsule.

1   2   3   4   5   6   7   8   9   10

In a typical week, I never consume enough polyphenols.

In a typical week, I sometimes consume enough polyphenols.

In a typical week, I always consume enough polyphenols.

5. Briefly review the numbers you circled for the five principles. Beginning with the principle you rated with the lowest number, use the action plan chart on page 155 to identify at least one thing you can do this week to increase your practice of all five principles. For example:

MY ACTION PLAN

ACTIONS I WILL TAKE	TIMEFRAME
Add fish (omega-3s) · Buy frozen salmon so I always have it as an option. · Set a recurring alert on my phone to remind me to take my fish oil supplements twice a day.	Saturday Today
Increase fiber · Eat a high-fiber cereal for breakfast. · Eat apple slices or fiber bars for snacks.	Tomorrow
Exercise · Email Chris and ask her to walk with me after work this week. · Visit the recreation center web site and sign up for an exercise class that starts within the next month.	Today Thursday
Reduce calories · Visit the web site for the restaurant where we'll eat out Friday night. Identify my healthiest option in advance. · Have hot tea rather than a latte when I meet Jill for coffee.	Thursday Monday
Increase nutrient-rich fruits and veggies · Visit the farmers market and pick up blackberries and grape tomatoes. · Put my green tea supplement on the kitchen counter so I remember to take it.	Saturday Today

After completing your chart, add your action items to your calendar. If taking actions in all five areas feels like too much for this week, circle the top two or three items you want to focus on and add those items to your calendar. Once you feel comfortable with those two or three practices, begin to add the additional items you identified to your weekly calendar.

After adding your action items to your calendar, use the guided prayer on page 156 or your own prayer to conclude your personal study.

MY ACTION PLAN

ACTIONS I WILL TAKE	TIMEFRAME
Add fish (omega-3s)	
Increase fiber	
Exercise	
Reduce calories	
Increase nutrient-rich fruits and veggies	

Guided Prayer

God,

Thank You for inviting me to grow closer to You through my struggles with food and healthy eating.

When I think back on all I've learned and experienced in the last several weeks, I am especially grateful for . . .

As I think about making a lifelong commitment to healthy eating, I know I will have to overcome many challenges. I especially need Your help with . . .

Thank You, Lord, for helping me to make courageous choices. I trust You to be my strength, to provide for me, and to lovingly guide me into becoming the person You made me to be. I love You, Lord. Amen.

Made to Crave DVD Curriculum

Satisfying Your Deepest Desire with God, Not Food

Lysa TerKeurst,
President of Proverbs 31 Ministries

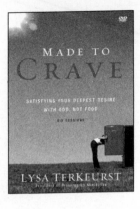

According to author Lysa TerKeurst, craving isn't a bad thing, but we must realize God created us to crave so we'd ultimately desire more of Him in our lives. Many of us have misplaced that craving, overindulging in physical pleasures instead of lasting spiritual satisfaction.

For a woman struggling with unhealthy eating habits, *Made to Crave* will equip her to:

- Break the "I'll start again Monday cycle" and start feeling good about herself today
- Stop beating herself up over the numbers on the scale and make peace with the body you've been given
- Discover how weight loss struggles aren't a curse but, rather, a blessing in the making
- Replace justifications that lead to diet failure with empowering go-to scripts that lead to victory
- Eat healthy without feeling deprived
- Reach a healthy weight goal while growing closer to God through the process

Made to Crave session titles include:
Session 1: What's Really Going On Here?
Session 2: Made for More
Session 3: Making Peace with the Realities of My Body
Session 4: God's Portion Control
Session 5: Emotional Emptiness
Session 6: Made to Crave—Made for Victory

The *Made to Crave* DVD is designed for use with the *Made to Crave Participant's Guide.*

Available in stores and online!

Becoming More Than a Good Bible Study Girl DVD Curriculum

Living the Faith after Bible Class Is Over

Lysa TerKeurst,
President of Proverbs 31 Ministries

"I really want to know God, personally and intimately."

Those words of speaker, award-winning author, and popular blogger Lysa TerKeurst mirror the feelings of countless women. They're tired of just going through the motions of being a Christian: Go to church. Pray. Be nice. That spiritual to-do list just doesn't cut it. But what does? How can ordinary, busy moms, wives, and workers step out of the drudgery of religious duty to experience a living, moment-by-moment, deeply intimate relationship with God?

In six small group DVD sessions designed for use with the *Becoming More Than a Good Bible Study Girl Participant's Guide,* Lysa shows women how they can transform their walk with God from lackluster theory to vibrant reality. The *Becoming More Than a Bible Study Girl* DVD curriculum guides participants on an incredible, tremendously rewarding journey on which they will discover how to:

- Build personal, two-way conversations with God
- Study the Bible and experience life-change for themselves
- Cultivate greater authenticity and depth in their relationships
- Make disappointments work for them, not against them
- Find incredible joy as they live out their faith in everyday circumstances

Sessions include:

1. Becoming More Than a Good Bible Study Girl ... in My Heart
2. Becoming More Than a Good Bible Study Girl ... in My Walk with God
3. Becoming More Than a Good Bible Study Girl ... in My Relationships
4. Becoming More Than a Good Bible Study Girl ... in My Struggles
5. Becoming More Than a Good Bible Study Girl ... in My Thoughts
6. Becoming More Than a Good Bible Study Girl ... in My Calling

Available in stores and online!